Gorbachev, Yeltsin, and Putin

Russia and Eurasia Books from
The Carnegie Endowment for International Peace

Belarus at the Crossroads
  Sherman W. Garnett and Robert Legvold, Editors

Getting It Wrong: Regional Cooperation and the
  Commonwealth of Independent States
  Martha Brill Olcott, Anders Åslund, and Sherman W. Garnett

Keystone in the Arch: Ukraine in the Emerging Security
  Environment of Central and Eastern Europe
  Sherman W. Garnett

Rapprochement or Rivalry? Russia-China Relations in a Changing Asia
  Sherman W. Garnett, Editor

Russia after Communism
  Anders Åslund and Martha Brill Olcott, Editors

Russia in the World Arms Trade
  Andrew Pierre and Dmitri Trenin, Editors

U.S.-Russian Relations at the Turn of the Century
  *Reports of the Working Groups organized by the Carnegie Endowment
  for International Peace and the Council on Foreign and Defense Policy*

Yeltsin's Russia: Myths and Reality
  Lilia Shevtsova

Gorbachev, Yeltsin, and Putin

Political Leadership in Russia's Transition

Archie Brown
Lilia Shevtsova
Editors

CARNEGIE ENDOWMENT FOR INTERNATIONAL PEACE
Washington, D.C.

Carnegie Endowment for International Peace
1779 Massachusetts Avenue, N.W., Washington, D.C. 20036
202-483-7600   www.ceip.org

The Carnegie Endowment normally does not take institutional positions on public policy issues; the views and recommendations presented in this publication do not necessarily represent the views of the Carnegie Endowment, its officers, staff, or trustees.

To order, contact Carnegie's distributor:
The Brookings Institution Press
Department 029, Washington, D.C. 20042-0029, USA
1-800-275-1447 or 1-202-797-6258
Fax 202-797-2960, E-mail bibooks@brook.edu

Printed in the United States of America on acid-free recycled paper with soy inks.

Typesetting by Oakland Street Publishing. Text set in ITC Berkeley.

Library of Congress Cataloging-in-Publication Data

Gorbachev, Yeltsin and Putin: political leadership in Russia's transition /
    Archie Brown, Lilia Shevstova, editors.
        p. cm.
ISBN 0-87003-186-4 (pbk. : alk. paper)
    1. Soviet Union--Politics and government--1985-1991. 2. Russia (Federation)--Politics and government--1991- 3. Political leadership--Russia (Federation) 4. Political leadership--Soviet Union. I. Brown, Archie, 1938- II. Shevtsova, Liliia Fedorovna, 1951- .
DK288 .G665 2001
947.086'092'2--dc21   2001004154

08   07   06   05   04   03   7   6   5   4   3   1st Printing 2001

Contents

Foreword, Jessica T. Mathews   vii
Preface   ix

1. Introduction   1
    Archie Brown

2. Transformational Leaders Compared:
    Mikhail Gorbachev and Boris Yeltsin   11
    Archie Brown

3. Evaluating Gorbachev and Yeltsin as Leaders   45
    George W. Breslauer

4. From Yeltsin to Putin: The Evolution of Presidential Power   67
    Lilia Shevtsova

5. Political Leadership and the Center-Periphery Struggle:
    Putin's Administrative Reforms   113
    Eugene Huskey

6. Conclusion   143
    Lilia Shevtsova

Index   153
Contributors   161
The Carnegie Endowment for International Peace   163

Foreword

The dramatic changes in Russia over the past fifteen years cannot be attributed exclusively to the decisions of political leaders, but the evidence presented in this book shows how foolish it would be to discount the difference new leadership can make even within systems that seem very set in their authoritarian ways. The transformational role of Mikhail Gorbachev and Boris Yeltsin, and the more ambiguous leadership of Vladimir Putin, are analyzed by four prominent analysts of Russian politics from three different countries. The authors—Archie Brown, George Breslauer, Eugene Huskey, and Lilia Shevtsova—have areas of disagreement as well as agreement, but they all bring to bear fresh and interesting perspectives based on long experience and solid research.

Whatever the shortcomings of the Russian political system today, it would be impossible to find anyone who predicted in 1985 that within less than five years Russia would be experiencing contested elections and freedom of speech. Sixteen years after the coming to power of Gorbachev, the liberty introduced during his years in power still, in the main, survives. Russian leaders have come to recognize competitive elections and a variety of freedoms as a necessary means for legitimizing their authority. Yet there are no grounds for complacency. Over the past two years the Russian mass media have come under renewed pressure. There have been signs in Russian society of a desire to find a new savior and of some nostalgia for the pre-reform Soviet system. Faith in what has passed for democracy in Russia has gradually declined, while public disillusionment with the behavior of those who style themselves democrats has increased.

The role of political leaders, not least Russian political leaders, in ending the Cold War has been well documented and is discussed in the pages that follow. With two new and relatively young presidents in both Russia and the United States, the relationship to be established between Vladimir Putin and George W. Bush will also have a profound impact on international relations. Even a weakened Russia is likely to be an important force for good or ill in a world that is in many ways less predictable than it was during the Cold War years. It would therefore be wise to attempt to reach a more profound understanding of contemporary developments in Russia.

The authors of this volume, all of whom have an impressive record as interpreters of Russian politics, provide new insight into Russian leadership politics during a time of transformative change. Notwithstanding some differences of emphasis, they are able to draw significant conclusions on the leadership of both Gorbachev and Yeltsin. In contrast, many questions concerning Vladimir Putin's future role remain open. Whether Russia will become a more or less democratic country depends on many factors apart from Putin's leadership, but the institutional power of the Russian president is such that his policy preferences and choice of priorities could tilt the balance one way or the other. The case for constructive engagement on the part of Western leaders with their Russian counterpart is, accordingly, a strong one.

Jessica T. Mathews
President, Carnegie Endowment
for International Peace

Preface

This book had its origins in a panel that met in Tampere, Finland, on August 3, 2000. It was convened by Archie Brown as a contribution to the VI World Congress of the International Council for Central and East European Studies (ICCEES) and chaired by Leslie Holmes. The presenters of papers and speakers at that panel were the four authors of the chapters that follow. The interest aroused by the panel, together with the significance of the theme to which it was devoted, convinced us that it would be worthwhile to present the product of our deliberations to a broader readership.

On Lilia Shevtsova's initiative, the Carnegie Endowment for International Peace was invited to consider publishing the resulting book. The four authors are grateful to Carnegie's readers, Thomas Carothers and Anatol Lieven, not only for their positive assessment of the manuscript but for their constructive suggestions; they also greatly appreciate the skilled in-house editorial work of Trish Reynolds and Sherry Pettie. It should be added that all of the Tampere presentations have been revised, expanded, and updated—in more than one case, very radically. Thus, the present volume takes account of developments and evidence available up to May 2001.

The publication of this book was made possible by grants from the Carnegie Corporation of New York, the Charles Stewart Mott Foundation, and the Starr Foundation, whose support is gratefully acknowledged.

The transliteration system adopted is a modified form of that used in the journal *Post-Soviet Affairs*. While Russian words are transliterated more strictly in the endnotes, the system has been adapted for the sake of read-ability in the main body of the text. There, for example, "skiy" endings in Russian names are simplified to "sky" (as in "Pulikovsky"), and "Aleksandr" appears as the more familiar "Alexander."

1

Introduction

Archie Brown

In an extremely hierarchical political system, which concentrates a great deal of power and authority in the top political office, the ideas, values, character, and style of the holder of that position acquire an especial significance. The Soviet system became strongly institutionalized, so that, particularly in the post-Stalin period, leaders too had to operate within a framework of constraints. Yet it is not for nothing that eras of Russian history are named after Lenin, Stalin, Khrushchev, Brezhnev, Gorbachev, and Yeltsin. The fifteen months spent by Yury Andropov and the thirteen months of Konstantin Chernenko as leaders (general secretary) of the Communist Party of the Soviet Union in the first half of the 1980s were too short—and, in the case of both of these men, too dogged by ill health—to merit such labeling. Nevertheless, the changes from Brezhnev to Andropov and then from Andropov to Chernenko were enough to produce a palpable difference of atmosphere that could be felt within Soviet society, as well as some difference of tone and style within the Soviet system.

Yet these were as nothing compared with the changes wrought by Lenin and Stalin or to be compared even with the boldness of Nikita Khrushchev in revealing and condemning at least some of the crimes of Stalin and thereby destroying the myth of the infallibility of the Communist Party. Khrushchev's aim, however, was to strengthen the authority of the party rather than to damage it, and he had some success in that endeavor—

notwithstanding the unintended consequences of his attack on the "cult of personality." Under Khrushchev, the Communist Party of the Soviet Union (CPSU) was rebuilt as a complex of powerful political institutions rather than as just one of the instruments of rule available to a dictator. The leading Western scholarly specialist on the CPSU, Leonard Schapiro, in what is still the major book on that organization, aptly entitled one of the chapters "Stalin's Victory over the Party."[1] Khrushchev himself, however, even though he had indeed revitalized the Communist Party, bypassed his colleagues when he deemed it necessary and took enough unilateral decisions that adversely affected powerful interests within the Soviet system for them to coalesce against him in 1964.

Leonid Brezhnev was not a leader of comparable boldness to Khrushchev, but it was precisely because he personified the interests of the *nomenklatura*, the senior officeholders in different branches of the Soviet establishment, that he gave his name to an age. Whereas Stalin had been a danger to the life and limb of officials even more than to ordinary workers, and whereas Khrushchev had been a threat to their peace of mind and security of tenure, Brezhnev's style, so far as intra-elite relations were concerned (the treatment of dissidents was an altogether different matter) was conciliatory and accommodating. This approach produced the nearest thing in the USSR to a golden age of the Soviet official—except, that is, for the younger and more ambitious among them, since Brezhnev's "stability of cadres" meant that promotion was slow and the Politburo turned into a gerontocracy.

There were plenty of reasons why an innovative policy should be pursued when, following the Andropov and Chernenko interregnum, a vigorous leader just turned 54 years of age, Mikhail Gorbachev, succeeded Chernenko as the sixth and (as it transpired) last general secretary of the Communist Party of the Soviet Union.[2] This is not the place to go into the numerous stimuli to change; they are touched upon in subsequent chapters of this book and have been widely and much more fully discussed elsewhere. But the buildup of problems does not in itself guarantee systemic change. There are enough regimes in the world that survive far longer than they deserve to, from a moral point of view, while remaining both politically oppressive and economically inefficient. Even for a *leader* to challenge the norms of a consolidated authoritarian state is unusual, for the risks of confronting established institutions within the system (not least that of the Soviet Union almost 70 years after the Bolshevik Revolution) are likely to be *far greater* than the risk of the system not surviving his time at the top of the political hierarchy. Cautious tinkering, in the Brezhnev manner, was more likely to see the leader still in office, and receiving fulsome tributes, until his death at an advanced age.

What, moreover, the experience of Khrushchev had shown was that the general secretary was by no means invulnerable. He could continue to enjoy an authority superior to all others within the system as long as he did not threaten or undermine the positions of the Soviet elite (or elites).[3] Gorbachev had gone well beyond Khrushchev's reforms in a great many respects. Moreover, he embodied and encouraged a different mentality from that of all previous Soviet leaders, ceasing to be any kind of Leninist even while he continued to accord Lenin as a politician more respect than was his due. Though an evolutionary rather than a revolutionary by temperament, Gorbachev launched both a conceptual revolution and an institutional reformation. They were transformative in ways both intended and unintended.

Freedom of speech and freedom from fear were enormous gains for Soviet and Russian society and for individual citizens, but given the accumulation of grievances, not least those of particular nationalities, the end to suppression of discordant voices provided the opportunity for separatist sentiment to gather support and for destabilizing forces to become stronger. The legitimation of a "pluralism of opinion" was reinforced by institutional changes that quite rapidly evolved into political pluralism. Similarly, Gorbachev's boldness in curtailing the power of the party apparatus, accelerated by the introduction of contested elections, undermined not only his own institutional base but also the structure that had played a huge part in holding together the multinational Soviet state. To allow federal forms to acquire federal substance—with the nominal authority of the component parts of the federation no longer filtered through, and constrained by, the single, centralized, ruling party—was to make the task of keeping all fifteen Soviet republics within the same political and legal space a Sisyphean challenge. In the end, the attempt to maintain this union on the basis of a looser federation or even confederation, and the effort to maintain by persuasion the territorial integrity of a state that had hitherto known only authoritarian or totalitarian rule, turned out to be a bridge too far even for such an exceptionally skilled bridge-builder as Gorbachev.

Both Gorbachev and Yeltsin, in their very different ways, took huge risks, although Gorbachev was also a master at "tranquilizing the hard-liners."[4] As Andrey Grachev, Gorbachev's former presidential press spokesman and a shrewd political analyst, has remarked: "People seldom ask how many coups d'état Gorbachev managed to avoid in six and a half years of reform."[5] It was crucially important that by the time the hard-liners awoke from their trance, they could no longer dispose of a leader as simply as they had removed Khrushchev. Both the system and the society had changed, and the conservative political forces that mounted the coup against Gorbachev with the aims of re-establishing the Soviet system he had been dismantling and of preserving the Soviet state they feared was disintegrating had been lulled into leaving things too late. Their actions in August 1991 merely speeded up the replacement of Gorbachev by Yeltsin and accelerated the breakup of the union.

Boris Yeltsin also, for better or worse (as is argued in the following chapter), played a huge part in breaking up the Soviet state. In the last years of the Soviet Union, he carved out for himself a position that hitherto had not existed in the USSR, that of Leader of the Opposition.[6] Yeltsin's finest hour, by common consent, was when he led the opposition to the hard-line coup of August 1991 from his base in the Moscow White House (which two years later he was to give the orders to bombard when it was occupied by his political enemies). But the legacy of Yeltsin's years in power was a hybrid political and economic system, combining substantial elements of democracy, arbitrariness, and kleptocracy. He was certainly a leader who made a difference, although he too was subject to constraints, albeit different constraints from those with which Gorbachev had to contend.

Vladimir Putin's inheritance from Yeltsin was a very mixed one. The freedom of speech and the press of the Gorbachev era had been maintained, some elements of democracy that emerged in the perestroika period had been given constitutional underpinning, and several fundamental economic changes had occurred under Yeltsin's leadership, most notably a substantial (though incomplete) price liberalization and the privatization of most commerce and much industry. However, on many indices—such as negative growth, capital flight, lack of industrial investment, demoralization of the armed forces, growth of corruption, increased alcoholism, and decline of public services (including deteriorating health care and a lowering of life expectancy)—the Russia Putin inherited from Yeltsin was in substantially worse shape than the Soviet Union of the perestroika years or, for that matter, the Brezhnev era.

In spite of the enormous differences between Gorbachev and Yeltsin, Vladimir Putin is in still more respects the odd one out in this trio of leaders of the Russia transition. Both Gorbachev and Yeltsin initiated change that broke radically with communist ideology and Soviet political practice, whereas Putin became a politician when the transition from communism had already taken place. Some observers see him as an agent of restoration of the old order, and he has made it clear that he shares with many Russians a nostalgia for the Soviet Union. This, however, Putin combines with the realism to accept that the former boundaries of a greater Russia in the form of the Soviet state cannot be restored. Furthermore, in principle at least, he supports party competition and pluralism in the mass media, even if some of the practice in these areas since he became president has caused serious worry to genuine democrats. In addition, while he has supported state ownership of the defense industry, he has categorically condemned proposals "to nationalize and confiscate property," arguing that it would lead to "arbitrary rule."[7] While Putin does not share Yeltsin's extreme distaste for the Communist Party of the Russian Federation and has been ready, unlike Yeltsin, to do deals with it in the course of his relations with the State Duma, he has also appositely remarked:

> Communists can either change their programmatic goals and become a major left-wing party of the European type, or they can take the other path and lose their social base through natural attrition. If they choose the latter, they will gradually exit the political stage.[8]

There is no doubt that Putin aims to restore Russian national pride, but restoration of communism is not on the political agenda. Equally, Putin aims to enhance the power of the central Russian state, but primarily so that its authority will be effective throughout the whole of its vast territory. While he clearly hankers after Russia's becoming again a great power (as distinct, though, from a superpower), he seems temperamentally averse to adventurism which would, in any event, be difficult in Russia's current straitened circumstances. Amidst the conflicting signals that have come from the Putin administration, perhaps the most important point to bear in mind is that Putin is an inexperienced leader who remains open to influence from both his domestic and foreign interlocutors. While he has described himself as "a pure and utterly successful product of Soviet patriotic education."[9] Putin has also discarded many of the beliefs he at one time took for granted.

It is too soon to determine whether Vladimir Putin will be a leader who makes a profound difference to the system and society he inherited. All the authors of the chapters that follow, though, are in agreement that both

Mikhail Gorbachev and Boris Yeltsin were transformational leaders, however much their evaluation of the two men's achievements and failures may differ in other respects. In a well-known book entitled *Leadership* written almost a generation ago, James MacGregor Burns distinguished between transactional and transforming leaders. The transactional leader works within existing norms and is a wheeler-dealer for whom reciprocity and adaptability are the essence of his or her leadership style—to such an extent, says Burns, "that leaders become hardly distinguishable from followers."[10] While not all leaders can readily be slotted into a neat dichotomy between the transforming and the transactional, and even transformational leaders have to know when to adapt and compromise as well as when to take bold initiatives, it is not difficult to fit Leonid Brezhnev and Konstantin Chernenko into the category of transactional leaders. For Burns, the notion of *transforming* leadership, in contrast with the transactional, has a moral dimension. It occurs when "one or more persons *engage* with others in such a way that leaders and followers raise one another to higher levels of motivation and morality."[11]

The authors of this book mean both more and, in some respects, less than Burns when they use the term "transformational" (rather than "transforming") leader. They have in mind not just leaders who *transform policy* (as in the case of Burns's paradigmatic transforming leader, U.S. President Franklin D. Roosevelt), but who are *systemic transformers,* whether we have in mind the political system, the economic system, or the international system. This is a much larger claim. However, while such leadership may, indeed, contain a moral dimension, system transformation does not necessarily go along with the elevation of followers and societies to a higher moral plane. Lenin was a transformational leader, par excellence, as was Stalin. Even though Stalin built on foundations laid by Lenin, he constructed a different system from the one Lenin had envisaged. The transformational character of their leadership can scarcely be doubted, but certainly none of the authors of this book and probably few of its readers would wish to commend the moral quality of their achievement.[12]

Another distinction to be found in the literature on leadership is that between leaders and managers.[13] Leaders, if they are to be effective, have to convey meaning and purpose and be much more than mere supervisors. Leadership that goes well beyond the transactional involves initiating change, creating a new agenda, and generating enthusiasm for it—as distinct from being content with the managerial outcome of predictability and order.

Effective leadership also involves developing political networks and communicating with those whose cooperation is necessary if change is to be implemented.[14] These are less demanding criteria than that of *systemic* change required by the transformational leader, and to varying degrees Gorbachev, Yeltsin, and even Putin meet them. The time dimension, though, has to be taken into account, for the content of the policies enunciated by Gorbachev and Yeltsin and the relative enthusiasm with which they were received varied over the years. It was especially during the first four of his six and a half years in power that Gorbachev was the initiator of change and only in his earliest years as Russian leader that Yeltsin was a real agenda-setter. Later in their political careers, both Gorbachev and Yeltsin found it harder to determine the political agenda and much more difficult to engender popular support for their policies. Sustaining coalitions or networks of influential insiders on whom they could rely also became increasingly problematical.

Nevertheless, of the three top leaders examined in this concise volume, two of them, Gorbachev and Yeltsin, in the terms expounded in subsequent chapters, are clearly *transformational* leaders.[15] Whether Vladimir Putin will be much more than a transactional leader remains to be seen. Yet, the institutional resources at the disposal of the Russian president, together with the traditional tendency to defer to higher authority, mean that Putin has, at least, more scope than anyone else in contemporary Russia to influence the direction taken by a transition whose point of departure is known and already consigned to history but whose destination remains unknown. The categories of transactional, on the one hand, and transforming/transformational, on the other, do not in any case fully embrace the distinctive importance of leadership at a time of systemic transition. When the norms governing political behavior have, along with established institutions, been cast aside for whatever reason, the choices made by leaders assume far more than usual significance. Since they are liable to have a disproportionate influence over the process of institutional design and institution-building, they may be making choices that will determine the structures and constraints of the evolving system for years to come. This has surely been the case in the late Soviet and post-Soviet periods of Russian politics.

Moreover, even when considering such transformational leaders as Gorbachev and Yeltsin, we need to distinguish which transformations we are talking about (a point I elaborate in chapter 2) and which criteria for evaluating these leaders we are applying (an issue elucidated by George

Breslauer in chapter 3). In chapter 4, we move from a pairing of Gorbachev and Yeltsin to a comparison of Yeltsin and Putin. Lilia Shevtsova traces the evolution of presidential power in post-Soviet Russia and examines to what degree Putin is making a break with the norms and institutions he inherited from Yeltsin. In the penultimate contribution to the volume (chapter 5), Eugene Huskey focuses on Putin's first year in the presidency, while paying due attention to its antecedents, and extends the scope of our concern with leadership by analyzing not only Putin's institutional innovations affecting the center's relations with the regions but also leadership in the regions themselves. While there is no doubt that a reassertion of central state power has occurred under Putin, his regional reforms—like so many reforms in Russia over the past fifteen years—could have unintended as well as intended consequences. In her concluding chapter, Lilia Shevtsova reflects on the leadership of Gorbachev, Yeltsin, and Putin and, although far from complacent about post-Soviet Russian political experience thus far, finds grounds for some guarded optimism about the future.

Notes

1. Leonard Schapiro, *The Communist Party of the Soviet Union* (London: Methuen, rev. and exp. ed., 1970), pp. 403–421.

2. Lenin was not general secretary of the party, but chairman of the Council of People's Commissars, i.e., head of the government. Although recognized as the country's leader, he was the exception to what became the Soviet rule. From Stalin's time until almost the end of the Soviet era—when an executive presidency was created in 1990—the general secretaryship was the key political position, the one that commanded most resources and whose holder exercised a superior power and authority to the heads of the Council of People's Commissars (later Council of Ministers), except for the years in which the general secretary himself took over the formal headship of the government, as both Stalin and Khrushchev did for a time.

3. Although it was, and remains, wrong to apply the adjective "pluralist" to the Soviet system and society any earlier than the late 1980s, it was a system in which there were different institutional interests. Among the major ones were the party apparatus (which had a superior authority to all the others), the ministerial bureaucracy, the military, and the KGB. Indeed, there was a diversity of interest even within these organizations, but they could come together to promote a common *nomenklatura* interest when they felt under threat, as they did (successfully) against Khrushchev in 1964 and (much less unitedly and less successfully) against Gorbachev in 1991.

4. Comparative study of transitions from authoritarianism suggests that this is a necessary phase in most democratization processes, not one specific to the Soviet Union. See Guillermo

O'Donnell and Philippe C. Schmitter, *Transitions from Authoritarian Rule: Tentative Conclusions about Uncertain Democracies* (Baltimore, Md.: Johns Hopkins University Press, 1986), p. 44.

5. Andrei Grachev, *Final Days: The Inside Story of the Collapse of the Soviet Union* (Boulder, Colo.: Westview Press, 1995), p. xi.

6. In pre-perestroika conditions it would have been impossible to play such a role, although in the Brezhnev era both Alexander Solzhenitsyn and Andrey Sakharov, notwithstanding their different political beliefs, stood out among the persecuted critics of the regime, their fame protecting them to some extent from the still worse treatment meted out to many of their fellow dissidents.

7. Vladimir Putin, *First Person* (London: Hutchison, 2000), p. 181.

8. Ibid.

9. Ibid., p. 42.

10. James MacGregor Burns, *Leadership* (New York: Harper & Row, 1978), p. 258.

11. Ibid., p. 20.

12. Lenin and, more especially, Stalin do not, accordingly, fit into Burns's category of transforming leaders, although they were clearly transformational leaders in the sense in which that concept is used in this book and on the common sense criteria that they not only presided over but consciously willed and implemented enormous changes in the systems they headed and the societies they governed.

13. See Barbara Kellerman, *Reinventing Leadership: Making the Connection Between Politics and Business* (Albany: State University of New York Press, 1999); and John Kotter, *A Force for Change: How Leadership Differs from Management* (New York: The Free Press, 1990).

14. See Kellerman, ibid., p. 148; and Kotter, ibid., p. 6.

15. In my own view, as chapter 2 makes clear, Gorbachev was a more comprehensively transformational leader than Yeltsin. See also Archie Brown, *The Gorbachev Factor* (Oxford: Oxford University Press, 1996), and Brown, "Mikhail Gorbachev: Systemic Transformer," in *Leaders of Transition,* ed. Martin Westlake (London: Macmillan, 2000), pp. 3–26.

2

Transformational Leaders Compared: Mikhail Gorbachev and Boris Yeltsin

Archie Brown

In comparing Mikhail Gorbachev and Boris Yeltsin as transformational leaders, we need to ask: *which* transformations? All too frequently a number of interrelated examples of profound political change are conflated into one "transformation" (or "transition") whereas the beginnings of a more rigorous analysis require that the different political phenomena be kept conceptually distinct. To delineate these transformations, and the roles or non-roles of Gorbachev and Yeltsin in each of them, is the first and main task of this chapter. It is followed by brief comparison of the two leaders on three different dimensions: 1) their style of rule; 2) sources of influence on them; and 3) interests and institutions supporting and constraining them.

First of all, then, we should make analytical distinctions among the following transformative changes: a) the Soviet Union's transition from "command polity" to political pluralism; b) the Soviet and Russian transition from command economy to a partly market and capitalist economy; c) the ending of the Cold War; d) the abandonment of communist regimes in Eastern Europe; and e) the breakup of the Soviet Union.

While there is not the slightest doubt that there is significant interlinkage among these important political phenomena, problems arise when, for example, the systemic transformation—a) and b) in the above categories—

is conflated with the breakup of the Soviet Union—category e). From 1988, Gorbachev was a systemic transformer in the sense that he had realized that reform of the Soviet Union was not enough and that the system, both political and economic, had to be comprehensively transformed. Yet neither then nor subsequently did he favor the disintegration of the Soviet *state* as distinct from changing the fundamentals of the Soviet *system*. On the contrary, no subject preoccupied him more during 1991, his last year in office, than the attempt to devise a union treaty acceptable to as many as possible of the republics of the Soviet Union. He saw his task by that time as preserving as much of the union as was feasible on the basis of voluntary agreement—or, to put it in "transitological" language, through a "pacted" settlement. The other way of holding the entire Soviet state together—resort to sustained coercion—he had rejected, but for Gorbachev the breakup of the USSR was very much an *unintended* consequence of perestroika (though *not*, he argues to the present day, a necessary consequence).[1]

Pluralization of the Soviet Political System

The pluralization of the Soviet political system—the creation of institutions that put an end to the command polity, including the monopoly of power of the Communist Party and "democratic centralism" within it—was more Gorbachev's doing than that of any other political actor. The system was such, *until* the Gorbachev reforms began to alter it, that no serious structural change could be undertaken by anyone other than the general secretary. Yeltsin, as a provincial party secretary, could either admire or silently oppose Gorbachev's initiatives, but could have no influence over them so long as he remained regional party boss in Sverdlovsk, and even his influence after he moved to Moscow in 1985 was to be far less than he desired. In fact, however, during the first two years of perestroika, Yeltsin did admire Gorbachev. Yeltsin's bodyguard and confidant, Alexander Korzhakov, maintains that as late as 1986 Yeltsin "worshipped" Gorbachev and rushed to take his telephone calls.[2] Over the course of 1987, however, Gorbachev called him less and less, and Yeltsin felt his support for Gorbachev was no longer being reciprocated. This distancing led to his famous, unscheduled speech at the October plenary session of the Central Committee that year and the break with the party leadership that was to be damaging to Yeltsin's career in the short term but was to stand him in wonderfully good stead later.[3]

When the pluralization of the Soviet political system was endorsed—however reluctantly on the part of a significant body of delegates—by the Nineteenth Party Conference in the summer of 1988, Yeltsin was still nominally a member of the Central Committee of the party, but completely marginalized. He played no part in the discussions that led to the adoption of the remarkably radical documents presented to the conference. The measures approved opened up political space which Yeltsin was soon to be astute and resolute in occupying. He was not only a prime beneficiary of the new pluralism but also someone who helped give it greater substance. Yeltsin's overwhelming victory in the 1989 elections for a seat in the new legislature—representing a constituency whose electorate embraced the whole of Moscow and facing an opponent, Yegveny Brakov, manager of the Zil car-manufacturing plant, who was the firm favorite of the Communist Party apparatus—was a landmark achievement. Yet, the U.S. ambassador to the Soviet Union at that time, Jack Matlock, appositely remarked: "I found Yeltsin's victory less astonishing than the fact that *the votes had been counted fairly*" (italics Matlock's).[4]

Gorbachev came to power in 1985 as a communist reformer, believing that the system could be substantially improved. Though from the outset he used the word *demokratizatsiya*—as well as perestroika (reconstruction), glasnost (openness or transparency), and *uskorenie* (acceleration)—what he had in mind between 1985 and 1987 is more aptly depicted as liberalization than democratization. His views, however, rapidly evolved, partly in response to the resistance that even modest reform encountered and partly as a result of the encouraging level of support he found he was able to elicit from large sections of the intelligentsia as they embraced glasnost and stretched its contours. Gorbachev was also influenced both before and after coming to power by his Western interlocutors and, on a more regular basis, by those close to him in the Soviet leadership as well as by his aides and advisers.[5] While the Politburo colleagues who were close to him in the early years of his leadership included a Yegor Ligachev as well as an Alexander Yakovlev and the aides included the later putschist, Valery Boldin, as well as the enlightened Anatoly Chernyaev, Gorbachev was himself in the vanguard, first, of reform and, then, of transformative change at least up to and including 1989. By then, political pluralism had been partly institutionalized through contested elections and enthusiastically supported by sections of the mass media. The system had become sufficiently different in kind that it was possible for the general secretary himself to be increasingly openly criticized—by radicals (among them Hayekian free marketers who, confusingly for their Western role models such as Margaret Thatcher, were in the Russian terminology of the time called "the left") as well as by conservatives (a term that, again to the dismay of Western conservatives, embraced unreconstructed, hard-line communists).[6]

It was in the run-up to the Nineteenth Party Conference that Gorbachev moved in 1988 from being a would-be reformer of the Soviet system to a systemic transformer. The introduction of contested elections for a new legislature, which was to meet during most of the months of the year and to have real powers (in contrast in both respects with the old Supreme Soviet), was a qualitative change in the political system. Gorbachev had to use the full weight of authority of the general secretaryship both to win the battle behind the scenes to introduce such a change and to prevent the deep misgivings of many regional apparatchiki from threatening its implementation.

Indeed, within the Politburo itself Gorbachev was in a minority in being willing to risk changing the fundamentals of the Soviet system, as was illustrated by the support of Viktor Chebrikov, Andrey Gromyko, Yegor Ligachev, Anatoly Lukyanov, Viktor Nikonov, Mikhail Solomentsev, and Vitaly Vorotnikov for what Gorbachev and Yakovlev called the "anti-perestroika manifesto" of Nina Andreyeva in March 1988. This was not, as it appeared superficially to be, a letter from an obscure Leningrad lecturer but an attempt, backed by conservative forces within the party's Central Committee, to reverse the radically reformist course on which Gorbachev had embarked. Showing none of the indecisiveness so often attributed to him, Gorbachev used to the full his personal and institutional authority to confront his more conservative colleagues and secure their "agreement" for the publication of a comprehensive rebuttal, drafted by Yakovlev, of views they actually shared.[7] Between 1988 and 1990, Gorbachev consciously moved political power from party to state institutions, and, having turned the danger posed by the Nina Andreyeva article into a political victory, he placed his reactionary and traditionalist opponents on the defensive throughout 1988–1989, the years in which the Soviet political system was changed fundamentally. Yegor Ligachev, who had begun as a conditional ally of Gorbachev but by 1986 was already showing the relatively narrow limits of his reformism and turning into a powerful brake on radical change, has summed up the position well, albeit from a position that viewed negatively Gorbachev's push for transformative change. Writing that "the process of transforming the electoral system accelerated too swiftly and radically," Ligachev goes on to say:

> To tell the truth, I already had my doubts about the need to rush through this law. But just recall the fall of 1988: there had been a powerful attack on me in connection with Nina Andreyeva's article, and I had more or less been removed from directing the Secretariat. Under those conditions it was difficult to speak out against the opinion of the general secretary and those who were clamoring for a maximum pace of political transformation.[8]

The role of Gorbachev in the transformation of the Soviet political system was put in still more pejorative terms by Vladimir Kryuchkov, who succeeded Chebrikov as chairman of the KGB in 1988 and who played a prominent part in the attempted coup of August 1991. In his memoirs Kryuchkov writes of Gorbachev: "His secret striving to destroy the CPSU was crowned with success because at the head of the party stood a traitor and, along with him, a row of his associates who were engaged in that treacherous cause."[9]

Transition from a Command Economy

The transition from a command economy has been a complex process and, although some elements of a market economy have been put in place in Russia, it would certainly be premature to say that a market system has already been established. If we are talking primarily about transition *from* a command economy as distinct from transition *to* a market economy, we can argue that the former transition was well under way during the perestroika period. The Law on Individual Labour Activity in 1986, the Law on the Enterprise of 1987, the Law on Co-operatives of 1988, and the Law on Leaseholds in 1989 all undermined, in ways both intended and unintended, the command economy. Moreover, the maxim that everything was permitted that the law did not specifically forbid was enunciated by Gorbachev and explicitly incorporated into much of this economic legislation.[10] The decentralization of power to enterprise managers initiated by the Enterprise Law and the boost to de facto private enterprise given by the Law on Co-operatives of the following year paved the way for much of the explicit privatization of the Yeltsin period.

However, though Gorbachev undoubtedly wished to move towards a mixed ownership economy and one with a market—albeit on the model of social democracy rather than American capitalism—the reality was that in 1990–1991 the economic system was in limbo. It was no longer a command economy, but empty shelves in the shops even of Moscow made clear just how far short of a market system it remained. The transition to a partially market economy and to a form of capitalism is an area of transformation where it can persuasively be argued that Yeltsin played a more decisive role than Gorbachev, with his support in 1992 for Yegor Gaidar's freeing of most prices and his subsequent support for Anatoly Chubais's privatization. The command economy was one of the pillars of communism that had been seriously undermined by Gorbachev but not yet completely toppled. It was finally overturned by Yeltsin, even though to describe what replaced it in post-Soviet Russia as a market economy would be an exaggeration. Just as Russia, after the fall of communism, has been a very partially democratized state, with a hybrid political system, so it has a hybrid economy, one that, in Joel Hellman's words, rests in "partial reform equilibrium."[11] Notoriously, privatization, in particular, has proceeded along lines that owed more to connections, cronyism, insider dealing, and exchange of political favors than to market forces.[12] One of the most serious analysts of Russia's travails among Western economists, Richard E. Ericson, has suggested that "economic institutions and interactions have settled into mutually consistent, self-reproducing expectations and patterns of behavior that are far from those consistent with a market economy" and that, indeed, Russia may not even be undergoing a "market transition," but creating instead a neo-feudal system that could turn out to be "as much an alternative to a modern market economy as was its predecessor, the Soviet command economy."[13]

What, of course, is beyond dispute is that, despite the continuing importance of *blat* (an informal relationship of exchange based on mutual favors), *svyazy* (connections), and the support of political power-holders—phenomena familiar from Soviet times—the economic mechanism works profoundly differently from the way it did even as recently as the late 1980s. In consumer goods there is a market that, in sharp contrast with the habitual Soviet shortages, means that everything is available, albeit at a price that tens of millions cannot afford. This particular transformation is very much Yeltsin's doing in the sense that he gave crucial political support to the "young reformers," enabling them to embark on the process both of freeing many prices and of speedy privatization. Moreover, Yeltsin went on to resist calls for the reversal of privatizations that had seen state assets sold off at a fraction of their true value. While admitting that the auctions, for example, of Svyazinvest, Norilsk Nickel, and Sibneft, with their rich pickings, were skewed in favor of particular buyers in advance, Yeltsin even in retrospect stood by the decisions that were made, saying: "Although many people wanted a review of the auction results, I was adamantly against it."[14] By giving that support to the privatization process, Yeltsin, by accident or design, helped to create economic groupings with a powerful interest in defending the "partial reform equilibrium." Whether to have presided over the introduction of a crooked form of capitalism is to Yeltsin's *credit* is a matter for value judgment. That it constitutes *transformative* change is less disputable. The system operates under different principles from those that governed the Soviet economy and is already a world away from the USSR's five-year plans and the heavy hand of central control in the shape of Gosplan and Gossnab.[15]

The Ending of the Cold War

Argument still continues over the role of the West—and, in particular, that of the Reagan administration—in bringing about the end of the Cold War, but two things, at least, are clear. The first is that the Cold War showed no signs of ending—on the contrary, it was getting colder—during the years in which the Reagan presidency overlapped with three other Soviet general secretaryships before Gorbachev entered the Kremlin in March 1985. The last two years of Leonid Brezhnev and the brief periods at the top of Yury Andropov and Konstantin Chernenko saw veteran Foreign and Defense Ministers Andrey Gromyko and Dmitry Ustinov conducting Soviet foreign and security policy inflexibly and responding to stepped-up military expenditure in the United States in traditional ways. It was Gorbachev who sanctioned, promoted, and established new thinking, new behavior, and a new foreign policy team in Moscow. The early replacement of Gromyko by Eduard Shevardnadze (in summer 1985) and the unprecedentedly fast-track promotion of Alexander Yakovlev—from not being even a candidate member of the Central Committee in 1985 to full membership of the Politburo and a secretaryship of the Central Committee in 1987—demonstrated

Gorbachev's intention to pursue an innovative foreign policy, which even Western skeptics were eventually forced to admit he carried through.

The second indubitable point is that the Cold War ended while Gorbachev was at the helm and his successor had no hand in that particular transformation. Yeltsin, even in the last years of the Soviet Union, did not have a foreign policy distinctive from that of Gorbachev and, moreover, made few pronouncements on the subject. His input into the foreign policy process was zero during the years in which East-West relations were transformed. Gorbachev's brilliant interpreter at summit meetings with U.S. presidents, Pavel Palazchenko, who is also a shrewd political observer, has noted that during the perestroika period Yeltsin took "little interest in foreign policy" and still less interest in the theoretical concepts that were embodied in what became known as the "new thinking."[16] Palazchenko, writing in the mid-1990s, continues:

> Yeltsin's main political strength is his unfailing instinct for power. In 1988–91 his road to power went through populist politics. He had a gut feeling for what the people wanted, and the people supported Gorbachev's foreign policy. There was therefore little that Yeltsin could do or say on foreign policy issues with a clear political benefit for himself.[17]

Even in the post-Soviet period Yeltsin did not so much determine as symbolize Russia's role vis-à-vis the outside world, only sporadically playing a decisive part. The main point in the present context, however, is that East-West relations had qualitatively changed before he entered the Kremlin. For George Shultz the Cold War was already over by the time he left office as secretary of state at the end of 1988.[18] By then Ronald Reagan and Gorbachev had signed important arms control treaties and Reagan had made his amicable visit to Moscow in the course of which he said that the Soviet Union was no longer an "evil empire."

Gorbachev, in contrast with Yeltsin, was genuinely interested in ideas. These included ideas on international relations whose conduct, so far as he was concerned, was no longer to be determined either by hidebound ideological preconceptions or by pure power politics. As Robert English, the author of a well-informed book on the development of the "new thinking" on foreign policy in the Soviet Union has noted, Gorbachev had an "insatiable thirst for knowledge" and this led him to read works that would not have appeared on the desk of most members of the Soviet *political elite* (as distinct from the policy advisory *academic elite* in the research institutes), including works of Western political science and the memoirs of Western politicians.[19] Even after he had become general secretary, and especially in the earliest stages of his leadership, in 1985–1986, Gorbachev broadened his already extensive reading still further. Western books that were not available to the ordinary Soviet reader (though very soon they would be as glasnost evolved rapidly into freedom of speech and publication) had for years been translated and printed in small and restricted editions for distribution exclusively to senior members of the *nomenklatura* (or for sufficiently trusted academics who were expected to engage in counter-propaganda against bourgeois ideology and who could read such works in the closed sections of major libraries). Even when he was a regional party secretary in his native Stavropol area of southern Russia, Gorbachev took advantage of these opportunities, and when, as general secretary, he found himself for the first time in his life having to take decisions on foreign policy, he continued to range well beyond Soviet orthodoxy in his reading matter. One of the important ways in which he made himself better informed was to encourage Soviet researchers to think the unthinkable and not to be afraid of rejecting the conventional wisdom in a country in which not being "politically correct" had traditionally had more dire consequences than in the West. Gorbachev likewise took the advice of others in the course of broadening his reading matter. As English observes:

> His wife, Raisa, introduced him to the integrationist, social democratic-leaning ideas of "semi-dissident" Moscow scholars. On policy matters, Arbatov offered the works of the Palme Commission and other European social-democratic writings on disarmament and "common security." With his interests now going beyond specific arms-reduction proposals to their underlying conceptions of international security, to the basic issues of survival, civilization, and human development on the eve of the twenty-first century, Gorbachev also reviewed writings from the Einstein-Russell manifesto of 1955 to the more recent works of the Pugwash scientists' movement.[20]

What was especially important, of course, was that Gorbachev's practice followed precept. Much of the rhetoric of traditional Soviet Marxism-Leninism concerning class struggle and proletarian internationalism had served as a rationalization of Soviet hegemony within the world communist movement and in the struggle between the two systems into which they saw the world as being divided. In contrast, Gorbachev's belief, influenced by his reading, that there were universal values and interests that transcended the differences between states became for him a guide to action—or, in the case of Eastern Europe, discussed in the next section, benign inaction.

The Abandonment of Communist Regimes in Eastern Europe

Against George Shultz's view that the Cold War was over by the end of 1988, a case can be made for saying that it was not truly over until the countries of Eastern Europe were allowed to choose their own political and economic systems, free from the controls and tutelage of Moscow. In 1988, first at the Nineteenth Party Conference in June and again at the United Nations in December, Gorbachev had declared such "freedom to choose." But it was Soviet non-intervention as one after another Central and East European country took him at his word in the course of 1989 that demonstrated beyond doubt that the Cold War was over.[21] The Cold War had begun with the Soviet takeover of Eastern Europe; it ended when a Soviet leadership— influenced both by new ideas of global interdependence and universal human interests and values and by a new calculus of the costs and benefits of maintaining Soviet hegemony over reluctant East European peoples— consciously decided no longer to sustain regimes that could not command the confidence of their own citizens. This decision was quickly felt by the East European communist leaders themselves. Károly Grósz, soon after succeeding János Kádár as Hungarian party leader in May 1988, sensed Gorbachev's lack of commitment to preserving the status quo in East-Central Europe. In an interview given in 1992, he said of Gorbachev: "Every time I asked him for something that I believed to be very difficult and delicate from the standpoint of Soviet interests in Hungary, he always said yes. I eventually came to the conclusion that he and Shevardnadze already had in mind a plan to completely disengage the Soviet Union from Eastern Europe."[22]

Gorbachev himself has been much criticized in Russia for ending the Cold War on terms disadvantageous to his own country. For many of his critics, that includes the abandonment of communist clients and pro-Soviet regimes in Eastern Europe. One of the most sophisticated book-length defenses of Gorbachev's policy on grounds of Russian national interest as well as morality is by Vadim Medvedev.[23] Gorbachev himself, in one of his more recent responses to the continuing barbs of nationalists and communist hard-liners, has written:

> Critics at home have also charged that we lost our allies in Eastern Europe, that we surrendered these countries without compensation. But to whom did we surrender them? To their own people. The nations of Eastern Europe, in the course of a free expression of the will of the people, chose their own path of development based on their national needs. The system that existed in Eastern and Central Europe was condemned by history, as was the system in our own country. It had long since outlived itself and was a burden on the people. Any effort to preserve this system would have further weakened our country's positions, discrediting the Soviet Union in the eyes of our own people and the whole world. Moreover, this system could have been "saved" in only one way—by sending in tanks, as we did in Czechoslovakia in 1968. The consequences of such unjustified action could have included a general European war.[24]

Here again we are dealing with an area in which Gorbachev—underpinned by the foreign policy team he appointed, consisting of Shevardnadze and Yakovlev (with successive heads of the International Department Anatoly Dobrynin and Valentin Falin playing a lesser role) and influential aides Anatoly Chernyaev and Georgy Shakhnazarov—was a truly transformational leader. In Western capitals it was still taken as axiomatic in the mid-1980s that Soviet hegemony over Eastern Europe was for Moscow nonnegotiable. The most that could be hoped for, and it was also the most that the East-Central Europeans themselves deemed to be feasible, was some relaxation and liberalization (of the kind that had occurred gradually in Kádár's Hungary) rather than full-fledged independence and the end of the Warsaw Pact, Comecon, and Soviet control. The reversal of the entire postwar Soviet policy towards Eastern Europe, as well as of other aspects of foreign policy, was conducted by Gorbachev within a narrow circle. Members of the Politburo and Central Committee were largely excluded, and the reformed Supreme Soviet was not an influential player in the foreign policy-making process. Falin, in his political memoirs, criticizes Gorbachev for failing to get the agreements with Germany ratified by the Supreme Soviet, although the extent to which his own advice and that of the International Department had ceased to have a major impact obviously rankled more.[25] In general, he blames Gorbachev for making far too many concessions to his overseas interlocutors in foreign policy.[26] Falin's immediate predecessor in charge of the International Department had felt much the same. Although Chernyaev described the former Soviet ambassador to Washington, Anatoly Dobrynin, as "very loyal and good-natured" and his relationship with Shevardnadze as "co-operative,"[27] Dobrynin was evidently nursing resentment about the subordinate role that was all he was allowed to play during the years, 1986–1988, when he headed the International Department. He complains in his memoirs that Gorbachev and Shevardnadze monopolized foreign policy making and of the fact that the International Department was "no longer involved in foreign policy on an everyday basis."[28]

The Breakup of the Soviet Union

The dissolution of the Soviet Union was in an important sense a transformation for which Gorbachev bears a large measure of responsibility even though it was an outcome he struggled desperately to avoid. But by embracing the liberalization and, then, the democratization of the Soviet political system, he allowed national discontents to come to the surface and to be articulated and defended. What was especially important in this context was the existence of Union Republican institutions which formed a basis for political mobilization along ethnic lines.[29] Once contested elections were introduced for republican legislatures, the arrows of accountability changed direction. It became more important for deputies to be responsive to, and have the support of, their local electorate than (as in the past) to curry favor with Moscow.

No less important, Gorbachev's readiness to let the "outer empire" go raised the expectations and nationalist consciousness of elites and a substantial part of the population in the most restive parts of the "inner empire." "Why," asks Jerry Hough, linking systemic transformation and the collapse of Soviet statehood, "did liberalization give way to Gorbachev's transformation of the system and lead to its destruction in such a short time? The immediate reason was that Gorbachev refused to use enough force to ensure obedience to Soviet laws and to suppress separatism."[30] The policy implication would appear to be a much more ruthless application of force to dampen down the slightest notion that a secession movement within the Soviet Union could emerge victorious. If such a policy had been applied before expectations were aroused—and it would have been no more than a continuation of a policy that had over many decades successfully prevented nationalist separatism from getting out of hand—the Soviet Union might indeed have been held together. But it would have been at a higher price than Gorbachev and the "new thinking" wing of the Soviet leadership were willing to pay.

Expectations of independent statehood for the fifteen Union Republics that made up the USSR were nonexistent when Gorbachev succeeded Chernenko. After all, if even Poles and Hungarians did not in 1985 imagine that within far less than a decade they would be living in a multiparty democracy, having shed their ties with Russia, and be awaiting membership in the European Union, still less did such far-fetched ideas cross the minds of Lithuanians and Estonians as the funeral of Chernenko took place. That Gorbachev bears some political responsibility for the breakup of the Soviet Union is, then, beyond doubt. In post-Soviet Russia he is, indeed, far more often blamed for applying insufficient coercion to hold the country together, a criticism Hough seems to endorse, than for the short-lived use of force (sometimes, as in Tbilisi in April 1989, in flat contradiction of Gorbachev's instructions)[31] that occasionally occurred. That is not to say that his reluctance to spill blood to preserve the union at any cost is to be deplored. Quite the reverse. It was surely morally right even if it did much to facilitate an outcome—the dissolution of the Soviet state—that Gorbachev struggled to avoid, using all the *political* means at his disposal. Gorbachev was, however, the first Soviet general secretary to appreciate that *means* are no less important in politics than *ends*. If the means of sufficient force to hold the union together had been applied, it would have been a different kind of union from that which Gorbachev wished to create and preserve, one in which the liberalization and democratization of the system would, as an inevitable consequence, have been put into reverse.[32] The coalition on which Gorbachev would have had to rely (for a short time— until they removed him for having put their regime and the unity of the Soviet state in mortal danger) would have been very different from that which he built for radical reform of the Soviet system.

There is an important sense in which Robert Conquest was right to call a democratized Soviet Union "a contradiction in terms." To the extent that the Soviet Union was democratized, it was clear that the Baltic peoples would use the newly available institutional means to demand independent statehood. That is not, however, to say that the majority of the Soviet republics might not have remained within a politically transformed, and genuinely federal, Soviet state had Yeltsin not played the Russian card against the union. If Gorbachev's responsibility for the breakup of the union consisted primarily of his embarking on liberalization and subsequently democratization, Yeltsin's was more direct: taking advantage of the new political climate to follow the lead of the Baltic states and to say that Russian law had supremacy over union law. The overwhelmingly greater part of the union could survive tiny Estonia declaring that its laws had supremacy over all-union legislation, but for Russia, with half the Soviet Union's population and three-quarters of its territory, to say the same was a devastating blow for those who wished to prevent the state's breakup.

In May 1990 Yeltsin stated that Russia had a right to "separate" from the union and that it could use such a right in "the same way that Lithuania had."[33] In the same month Yeltsin announced that union law should not contravene Russian legislation, for the latter had supremacy, and that Russia was taking possession of all natural resources on its territory.[34] From that time, Yeltsin pitted Russia against the union and in successive negotiations over a new union treaty was increasingly reluctant throughout 1991 to recognize that there was a place for a Soviet state as distinct from a loose multinational association. The future of the state was subordinated to personal ambition, not just that of Yeltsin but of many of his associates. They wished to remove the Gorbachev team from the Kremlin and install their own team in its place. Gorbachev was caught in a pincer movement, for in 1990 he also had reluctantly to allow a Communist Party of the Russian Republic to be formed and whereas Yeltsin, as chairman of Russia's Supreme Soviet, was attacking him in the name of speedier democratization, the Russian Communist Party under its leader Ivan Polozkov attacked him and his allies from a conservative communist position. To some extent, both the leadership of the Russian Communist Party and the leadership of the Russian Supreme Soviet represented what Andrey Grachev has called "the revolt of the second secretaries." There was not only a growing political pluralism within the society but also a pluralism of elites—and increasingly bitter rivalry among them. Their formation changed as some people moved from one camp to the other, especially from Gorbachev's to Yeltsin's during 1990–1991.

One of the best and most judicious of analyses of "causes of the collapse of the USSR" was by the late (and greatly missed) Alex Dallin.[35] He identified a number of major causes of change in the Soviet Union and rightly cautioned against introducing "retrospectively a clarity, let alone inevitability, where there was contingency and complexity."[36] Nevertheless, pointing to Yeltsin's actions from the declaration of Russian sovereignty in 1990 to the meeting with the Belorussian and Ukrainian presidents in December 1991 at which, together, they wound up what was left of the union without troubling themselves with legal process, he remarks that identifying Yeltsin "as the final catalyst" of the collapse of the Soviet Union "may be the easiest part of this exercise."[37] If Gorbachev, contrary to his objectives and as an unintended consequence of political transformation, left ajar the door to national separatism, Yeltsin opened it wide and eventually led Russia through it. Yet the argument that Russia was somehow thereby gaining its "independence" was much less plausible than in the cases of Estonia, Latvia, and Lithuania, for Russia and Russians had been the dominant partners within the most powerful all-union institutions for decades.

It was not, therefore, preordained that, as part of Yeltsin's struggle against Gorbachev, Russia should follow the example of the Balts and turn against the union, itself a successor to a Greater Russia which had existed for centuries. Tactically, by so doing, Yeltsin "momentarily united democrats and nationalists,"[38] and in terms of maximizing his own power within the political space of what was the RSFSR and is now the Russian Federation, it worked.[39] It *was*, indeed, a transformation, though whether it was one that promoted more than it retarded the development of democracy throughout the whole of the political space occupied by the former Soviet Union must remain in doubt at a time when there are more authoritarian regimes than democracies among the fifteen Soviet successor states. *Pace* Leon Aron and countless other authors, it also did *not* mean that Yeltsin "dissolved the Russian empire."[40] There are territories still within the Russian Federation, of which Chechnya is the most obvious example, that were much more recent imperial acquisitions than some of the lands that separated from Russia in 1991. In the case of Chechnya alone, far more bloodshed and indiscriminate destruction were sanctioned by Yeltsin than were permitted by Gorbachev even if one adds together all of the manifestations of national discontent and independence struggles of the entire perestroika period.

Style of Rule

Yeltsin continued to compete with Gorbachev for some time after the first and last Soviet president had ceased to be a major political actor in Russia. Yeltsin resented the fact that he did not achieve the international acclaim that had been accorded Gorbachev for the latter's part in transforming both the Soviet Union and international politics. As a group of Yeltsin's closest aides have divulged, he supported an atmosphere of "Gorbyphobia" in his milieu.[41] They note Yeltsin's jealousy of Gorbachev, not least when he continued to be very well received abroad after he had left office and when, in the course of those foreign visits, he was frequently critical of his successor's policies.[42] Yeltsin launched a fresh campaign against Gorbachev in 1992, by which time he had all the levers of executive power under his control. Thus, for example, he telephoned Minister of Interior Viktor Yerin and told him to carry out a "financial and legal inspection of the Gorbachev Foundation."[43] This order was duly obeyed and became just the first in a series of attacks on Gorbachev and his foundation which, however, never led to the closure of that institute—partly, no doubt, because Yeltsin's campaign against Gorbachev was badly received by those same Western leaders the Russian president was trying hard to impress.

For a time, and in the minds of some to the present day, Yeltsin had the reputation of being a more sincere democrat than did Gorbachev. Yet his political style vis-à-vis subordinates was always more authoritarian. Whether as regional party boss in Sverdlovsk or as Communist Party first secretary in Moscow or as Russian president, Yeltsin demanded absolute loyalty.[44] He also became more authoritarian and more inaccessible as time went on.[45] Even those who served him loyally have recorded that Yeltsin was chronically suspicious and also capricious. Sporadically, he could be a good listener, but those times became less frequent during the years of his presidency and, as with Leonid Brezhnev in his later years, his aides and senior officials found it virtually impossible to bring him bad news. He received it angrily and his daughter, Tatyana Dyachenko, was latterly the only person who could report failures to him.

Those who have worked with Gorbachev have come up with contradictory accounts of his leadership style. Georgy Shakhnazarov, who collaborated exceptionally closely with Gorbachev, has said that in all those years he never saw him lose control of his emotions or witnessed him being rude to subordinates. Others, such as the interpreter, Viktor Sukhodrev (who may have resented his replacement by Pavel Palazchenko) and even Anatoly Chernyaev have complained that Gorbachev took their service for granted. Sukhodrev compared Gorbachev unfavorably in that respect to Brezhnev who always thanked the interpreters for their services, whereas Gorbachev treated them as "part of the furniture, like tables, chairs or pencils."[46] (Palazchenko, who has worked for fifteen years as Gorbachev's principal interpreter, takes an altogether more positive view of him. Indeed, his memoirs constitute a sophisticated defense of Gorbachev's style and policies, even though he expresses disagreement with a number of his decisions.) Some of Gorbachev's collaborators, such as Alexander Yakovlev, say that in the earlier years when they worked with him, he was an exceptionally good listener, but later he talked more and listened less. The testimony *both* to Gorbachev as a "good listener" and to his talking too much is voluminous. Certainly, in interviews and speeches, Yeltsin's terseness, in the period when he was engaged in a struggle for supremacy with Gorbachev, counted to his advantage in comparison with Gorbachev's prolixity. Against that, Gorbachev had the superior intellect and never less than a clear head in contrast with the later Yeltsin's often slurred incoherence, again reminiscent of the last years of Brezhnev.

Gorbachev's greater tolerance and intellectual self-confidence were reflected in the fact that people could remain his aides over many years even though he had read their criticism of him in print. Thus both Chernyaev and Shakhnazarov, though fundamentally on Gorbachev's side, are by no means uncritical of him in their memoirs. Chernyaev, in particular, in his published diary extracts, expresses his exasperation at times. And Shakhnazarov, in his analytical reminiscences, in spite of extolling Gorbachev's many merits, describes him as "a bad organizer." When that book (*Tsena svobody*) was published in 1993, Gorbachev (as I was told by Shakhnazarov) argued with him and asked how could he be a poor organizer when he had held one important administrative post after another as he rose up through the party hierarchy in Stavropol and Moscow, being given ever-greater responsibilities? The relevant point here is that Gorbachev was prepared to try to persuade Shakhnazarov that his view was mistaken, but that he did not express outrage or anger. The idea of banishing Shakhnazarov from the inner circle never arose, and he remained to the day of his death at the Gorbachev Foundation.[47] It would be difficult to imagine aides continuing to work closely with Boris Yeltsin if Yeltsin read their description of him as a "bad organizer." Indeed, Korzhakov has written that the most important criterion for Yeltsin in appointing someone (ahead, for example, of professionalism) was that they should never have spoken a word against him.[48]

If one compares Gorbachev's and Yeltsin's relations with the public, Yeltsin had the more populist style and in the last two years of Gorbachev's leadership became much the more popular of the two leaders. He had also been more willing in those years to fight contested elections, though it is of considerable relevance that he had more incentive to do so. Gorbachev already occupied the highest political office in the land. Yeltsin, having boldly clashed with the Communist Party establishment of which he had been a part, in the autumn of 1987, had largely burned his bridges so far as a more traditional Soviet path to power was concerned. As late as 1988 he believed, nevertheless, that he could do little or nothing without being reinstated in the top party leadership team. At the Nineteenth Party Conference in that year he pleaded for "party rehabilitation," even though he was still, nominally, a member of the Central Committee of the Communist Party, albeit already ousted from his executive party posts. Yeltsin's political instincts, which often stood him in good stead, meant however that by the following year he had realized that running *against* the party apparatus could be maximally advantageous to him. He seldom disguised his ambition and, given his aspiration to become Russia's number one politician, he had everything to fight for.

If it was unique at that time, and to Yeltsin's credit, that a man from the party apparatus should decide in 1989 that his route to the top lay through the ballot box, it was only after the decisions Gorbachev persuaded the Nineteenth Party Conference to adopt—most specifically, the decision to move to contested elections—that *anyone* could have chosen that option for political advancement. Prior to those fundamental reforms of the previous year, the ballot box (with the name of a single candidate on the voting paper, and even that person's name there only after he or she had received the stamp of approval of the party authorities) would not have done Yeltsin or anyone else any good. Gorbachev's electoral reform, in conjunction with freedom of speech and, increasingly, of publication, had however opened up political space for rivals, of whom Yeltsin was to become the most formidable.

The contrast between Yeltsin's style when meeting the general public and Gorbachev's is not as great as is often suggested. In the early years Gorbachev—as, for example, in Leningrad in 1985—engaged in enormously popular walkabouts and conversations with groups of citizens who were not handpicked and stage-managed as they would have been in the days of Brezhnev. Gorbachev did not, of course, as general secretary attempt to emulate some of Yeltsin's more populist gestures, such as taking well-publicized occasional trips on municipal buses and the Moscow metro. In their later years in office both men had less spontaneous contact with the public, though Yeltsin took to the hustings again in 1996 and, with almost the entire mass media behind him, pulled off an impressive victory in an election that was presented to the public as a choice between him and a return to the communist past (with television programs on the Gulag and all the worst aspects of Soviet rule in generous supply to rub the point in).

Gorbachev himself, by this time a private citizen excluded from the political process, quixotically became a candidate in that election. Whereas in 1989 he had been by a large margin the most popular public figure in Russia, seven years later he was thoroughly marginalized and received less than 1 percent of the popular vote. Almost ignored by the mass media and finding many factories and meeting halls closed to him, following a telephone call from the presidential administration, he nevertheless campaigned across Russia—perhaps stung by taunts that his not standing for popular election when he was in power meant that he was afraid to do so. Ignoring on this occasion the advice of his most trusted advisers, including even that of his wife, Raisa (who, nevertheless, characteristically accompanied him on all his travels to Siberia and around the country),[49] Gorbachev had very close contact indeed with the section of the electorate he was able to meet, dealing bravely with hostile demonstrations and often winning over initially skeptical audiences in meetings that went largely unreported. During his years in power, however, his persuasiveness had been shown to greatest effect in his dealings with the major political institutions, including the new legislature, the Central Committee, and the Politburo when he succeeded in getting the Soviet political elite to accept changes that threatened the interests and went against the conditioned reflexes of most of them. Gorbachev, however, took especially seriously the legislature elected in 1989, the Congress of People's Deputies of the USSR and its inner body, the Supreme Soviet, and spent a vast amount of time attending (and initially chairing) its debates. In contrast, Yeltsin treated with a good deal of disdain both the legislature he had inherited from the Soviet period (which he forcibly disbanded in 1993) and its successor, the State Duma.

Sources of Influence

There are some similarities in the range of influences on Gorbachev as general secretary and on Yeltsin as Russian president, as well as striking differences. Both were influenced by people with ideas for radical reform, at one extreme, and by people from the security organs or "power ministries," at the other. Apart from the committed reformers Gorbachev brought into his immediate circle—Yakovlev, Chernyaev, and Shakhnazarov being among the most important examples—he listened to a wide range of reformist and critical opinion. Social scientists such as Abel Aganbegyan and Tatyana Zaslavskaya in the earliest period of perestroika and, later, economists Nikolay Petrakov and Stanislav Shatalin were among those who had the ear of Gorbachev; Petrakov even worked as an aide to Gorbachev throughout 1990. Radicals within their own generation, they were to be regarded as *insufficiently* radical by the "young reformers" embraced by Yeltsin, though their response to the dismissive remarks of a younger generation was that their commitment to the market was tempered by a deeper knowledge of Russian society and with the contention that the supposed reforms of Gaidar and Chubais suffered from disregard of social context and social consequences.

Gorbachev listened to a far wider range of advice than did Yeltsin. This was partly because, unlike Yeltsin, he did not have periods of lethargy and drinking, in which very little work was done and partly because of his greater interest in ideas. Gorbachev was the more intellectual politician (although that went along with political antennae finely attuned to the balance of forces and the limits of the possible at any given time within the Soviet ruling circles), while Yeltsin was the more instinctive and inclined to act on hunch. Yeltsin's conversion to the idea that the market economy was desirable was the banal experience of seeing a Western supermarket for the first time. From that it was but a short step for him to put his trust in young economists who were committed marketeers, especially Yegor Gaidar. Gaidar himself picks out Yeltsin's "intuition," especially his ability to sense the public mood, as his most important political quality.[50] But he notes that Yeltsin had other characteristics that were less useful in the conduct of state business. He found it far easier to convey sincere friendship or to engage in sharp confrontation than to display "subtle, complex feelings."

If Yeltsin's team contained people who were personally loyal (those who proved disloyal, such as Alexander Rutskoy and Ruslan Khasbulatov, were cast aside and demonized), it also at all times contained a wide range of views: those who were in favor of much more state regulation of the economy (such as, for a time, Oleg Lobov and Alexander Korzhakov, the latter over some years surprisingly influential for one whose formal position was that of chief bodyguard), as well as those such as Gaidar, Chubais, and Boris Fedorov who took a very different view. In that respect, there is some similarity with Gorbachev's leadership team in which there was tension throughout 1990 between the views on the market and the state of Nikolay Petrakov, on the one hand, and Nikolay Ryzhkov, on the other. The top leadership team contained reformers such as Yakovlev, Shevardnadze, and Medvedev, at the same time as relative conservatives such as the successive heads of the KGB, Chebrikov and Kryuchkov, and representatives of the armed forces and defense industry, Yazov and Baklanov.

There were times when Gorbachev took too seriously the biased information he was fed from the KGB, either directly by Kryuchkov or through his ally (and disloyal Gorbachev client Boldin), whether on the risk of civil war in Lithuania or on the dangers of a massive, and peaceful, demonstration in Moscow in early 1990. Latterly—from the time he launched the Novo Ogarevo process in April 1991—Gorbachev was paying scant attention to the fears of Kryuchkov, Baklanov, and company, and he negotiated a version of the union treaty that they believed would lead to the breakup of the Soviet Union. It was a sign of their lack of influence in the months between April and August 1991 that they resorted to the desperate measure of putting Gorbachev under house arrest on August 18 and announcing the next day the creation of the State Committee for the State of Emergency, thereby making their own unwitting contribution to the acceleration of the dissolution of the Soviet state.

Yeltsin took in a more limited range of information than Gorbachev, partly because he was prone to passivity and depression once an immediate goal had been attained.[51] It was important that he thought of himself as a "democrat," even if his understanding of democracy was limited. His definition involved a belief in contested elections but included little regard for most of the procedural and institutional aspects of democracy.[52] Indeed, even his commitment to elections was tempered by the rather important qualification that it must be an election that he could win. On his own admission, Yeltsin came very close indeed to canceling the 1996 presidential election at a moment when he felt that he was likely to lose. At that same time he had already ordered his staff to prepare decrees to dissolve the

Duma and to outlaw the Communist Party of the Russian Federation, the largest political party in the country. At a very late stage in the process Yeltsin was persuaded—on his own account by his daughter, Tatyana, and by Anatoly Chubais, although the opposition of Minister of Interior Anatoly Kulakov may have been more important—that this course of action would be imprudent and that, with sufficient resources behind him, he could fight the presidential election and win.[53] Within his entourage there were people (such as, for a time, Vyacheslav Kostikov) who tried to keep him in touch with those who thought of themselves as democrats, but with diminishing returns as the years went by, for his "court" (as Oleg Poptsov, among others, has called it) also contained people whose contempt for democrats was palpable. Latterly, Yeltsin had been deserted by many of the "democrats" in a manner somewhat reminiscent of Gorbachev's experience during his last two years in office.

Constraining and Supporting Institutions and Interests

That leads, finally, to a brief consideration of the different institutions and interests that constrained or supported Gorbachev and Yeltsin. Gorbachev had both the advantage and disadvantage of leading a ruling party. It was an advantage in some respects inasmuch as the leader of the Soviet Communist Party could rely on deference and respect. In the post-Stalin period he was far from a dictator, but his views carried more weight than that of anyone else in the Politburo. There was also a network of institutions capable of putting policy into effect. That, however, only held good so long as the rules of the game of the system were preserved. A general secretary who threatened the security of the party apparatus (as Nikita Khrushchev discovered) could be overthrown, and Gorbachev was very conscious of his predecessor's fate. Since Gorbachev was turning Marxism-Leninism upside down to a greater extent than Khrushchev ever did, introducing much more fundamental systemic change at home and taking far bolder and more heterodox foreign policy initiatives, he had to show exceptional skills of persuasion and placation of the party apparatus until such time as he had weakened the very structures through which he rose to power.

Gorbachev was also constrained, to some degree, by the military-industrial complex and the security organs. Brezhnev believed that he would have been overthrown if he had allowed the "Prague Spring" to proceed without

Soviet military intervention.[54] Gorbachev survived the "loss" of the whole of Eastern Europe but could scarcely be confident that he would be allowed to remain in office following the loss of parts of the Soviet Union. Thus, at a time when he was under great pressure from national independence movements in several republics, supported by radical democrats in Moscow, he was under no less intense pressure from those within the party and state establishment to defend the integrity of the Soviet state with all the means, including military, at his disposal. The conservative forces appeared, in the most literal sense, to have the big battalions on their side, and it is hardly surprising that the policy Gorbachev pursued on the "national question" should have been a compromise.

By creating the presidency, Gorbachev freed himself from such constraints as the party leadership and apparatus had been able to impose on him, though—as a result of his political skill—those constraints had been far less effective than they might have been. That was partly because Gorbachev, with the help of Yakovlev, summoned into existence, as it were, countervailing forces by encouraging glasnost and a developing freedom of the press, so that public opinion became a factor in Soviet political life as never before, especially intelligentsia opinion. Eventually, of course, this worked to Gorbachev's disadvantage. The balancing act of being both Pope and Luther, leader of the ruling party and leader of the opposition to the traditional policies of that party, left him in a position where he was liable to be outflanked and outbid from the radical "left" or overthrown by the conservative "right." In the event both things happened to him, though the latter was short-lived. Crucially, the attempt to oust Gorbachev did not occur until after he had guided through a system hitherto remarkably impervious to far-reaching political reform transformative change of that system.

Yeltsin had the advantage and disadvantage of *not* belonging to a party from the time he resigned from the Communist Party in the summer of 1990. Leading a ruling party both constrains and empowers a political actor. If it is a serious party, then the leader must listen to party colleagues and sometimes make concessions to views with which he or she disagrees. To change the fundamentals of party policy is not an easy task for a leader within a democratic state and it was not a straightforward matter within the oligarchical Soviet system. However little power the rank-and-file party member had, members of the Politburo and Secretariat, the Central Committee apparatus, and the regional party secretaries were political actors to be reckoned with. Yeltsin had seen such a system from the inside, and along with his growing disenchantment with the Communist Party went a desire to be free from the constraints that any party was liable to impose on its leader. The rationalization that a president must be the president of all the people was a very weak one, given that presidents in democracies find no difficulty in combining party affiliation with precisely such an understanding that they are the president for all citizens once in office.

Yeltsin did, however, suffer from other constraints. If one makes the assumption that Yeltsin was against the outflow of capital from Russia, it is worth noting Gaidar's complaint that the state security organs were not cooperative in efforts to investigate CPSU capital flight.[55] Yeltsin had, for a time, the support of radical democrats who had become disillusioned with Gorbachev, but not all of them turned out to be capable of administering anything more than a university department—a case in point being Gavriil Popov, Luzhkov's predecessor as mayor of Moscow. Thus, Yeltsin turned to "experienced cadres," including some who had worked with him in Sverdlovsk, for administrative support, and their mode of thinking was its own constraint. Famously, or notoriously, Yeltsin had the support of the mass media when it most mattered: during 1996 when he fought his second presidential election. More generally, the symbiotic relationship between financial-industrial groups and the Kremlin administration was both a constraint and a support for Yeltsin, although some parts of the media—most notably the Media Most group and its television channel, NTV—became much less uncritical once what they had perceived as the communist threat had been rebuffed. The financial resources of those who controlled the mass media and the media themselves were put to service in Yeltsin's cause, both as a way of protecting the assets of the media magnates and as a way of enhancing their political influence. For much of Yeltsin's presidency the support of the new class of "oligarchs" helped to preserve him in power, but this came at a political price. Unless it be assumed that Yeltsin did not care if the Russian state was deprived of revenues as a result of the sale of vital assets at knock-down prices (which, together with the failure of the new rich to invest in their own country, was enormously damaging to the Russian economy), the relationship of Yeltsin with business interests, and the latter's access to and even permeation of his innermost circle, must be seen as crucially constraining his freedom of action as well as casting serious doubt on his claims to have deepened the democratic process in Russia.

Conclusions

Boris Yeltsin, from the adoption of the December 1993 Russian Constitution onwards, had a strong executive presidency embedded in the political system. His frequent absences from political activity meant that he used his powers to the full only sporadically, but constitutionally he was in a strong position and he benefited also from the habits of mind in Russian political life whereby supreme authority was assumed to lie with the top leader rather than being dispersed among a variety of co-equal institutions. Mikhail Gorbachev had earlier been in the more paradoxical situation that the de facto power and vast authority of the Soviet general secretary—which was not even written into the Rules of the Communist Party of the Soviet Union, still less the Soviet Constitution—depended on the persistence of the power of that party within the political system. Yet that system was becoming pluralistic not only under Gorbachev's leadership but also with his decisive support, and he was replacing the unquestioned power of a publicly united Communist Party with representative institutions and a party that was in the process of dissolving into very different political groupings. Thus, if maximizing his length of time in office had been Gorbachev's overwhelming concern, he acted against his own interests. In reality, while Gorbachev did strive to remain in office, he was not prepared to seek power at any price, and power for its own sake—pulling traditional levers while presiding over an unreformed Soviet system—had no appeal for him.[56]

I have considered the parts played (or not played) by Gorbachev and Yeltsin in relation to five politically interrelated but analytically distinguishable transformations. From this comparison Gorbachev emerges as much the more significant transformational leader of the two. It was he who broke the Soviet mold and had the courage to embark on far-reaching reform. He did this not only from a pragmatic desire to improve Soviet economic performance (in which endeavor, in any event, he was unsuccessful) but because he retained ideals and possessed an optimism that a better society—specifically a humane and democratic socialism—could be built on Russian soil. Gorbachev's optimism was both innate (an integral part of his personality) and based on observation (especially what he had seen of Western Europe and his reading of works that had challenged Soviet Marxist-Leninist orthodoxy). In many respects, of course, Gorbachev's optimism turned out to be misplaced. The Russian economy was in worse shape in 1991 than in 1985, though it is worth adding that, on most indicators, it is even worse in 2001 than in 1991, not to speak of 1985. The other most striking gap between the aims and the results of Gorbachev's radically reformist efforts was the splitting apart of the Soviet Union. That was the last thing in Gorbachev's mind when he became general secretary. He himself was partly Ukrainian, on his mother's side, and his wife's father was Ukrainian. He truly believed in a multinational union and was convinced, again over-optimistically as it turned out, that it could be preserved on a new, voluntary basis and through turning what had been essentially a pseudo-federation into a genuine federation.

For the instinctive, noncerebral politician, Yeltsin, it is harder to say what he believed in. A number of those who have worked with him have come up with the same formula to describe his core belief and have said that *power* is Yeltsin's ideology. While that contains a very large element of truth, it is not quite the whole story. It would be hard to reconcile Yeltsin's criticism of the party hierarchy—and, in particular, of Yegor Ligachev—in October 1987 with that generalization. A little more than two years into perestroika, it was, to say the least, far from obvious that Yeltsin's flouting of Communist Party convention was the most obvious path to power. Yeltsin was nevertheless someone who, on his own admission, strove to be number one, hated being a subordinate, and chafed in particular under his subordination between 1985 and 1987 to Ligachev. It was Ligachev who had urged Gorbachev to bring Yeltsin from Sverdlovsk to Moscow as head of a department of the Central Committee and who later pressed his claims to be first secretary of the Moscow City organization of the Communist Party. He had unwisely, however, assumed that Yeltsin would thereby be "his" man, but Yeltsin, notwithstanding his earlier enthusiastic support for Gorbachev, would ultimately be only his own man. In that sense, he had undoubted qualities of leadership, including a decisiveness when his interest was aroused that frequently spilled over into impulsiveness.

If we sum up the five transformations, Gorbachev played the decisive role in the first—the pluralization of the Soviet political system. He liberalized the system and, from 1988, embarked on a process of democratization. That is not to say that Russia or most of the Soviet Union was a democracy by the end of the Soviet era, but nor is it a democracy today. It was between 1989 and 1991 a hybrid system: no longer communist in any meaningful sense of the term, but not having completed a transition to democracy.[57] However, it was a hybrid system with very substantial elements of democracy which Yeltsin inherited from Gorbachev. (Ten years on a hybrid system, albeit one composed of different elements, was what Yeltsin bequeathed to Vladimir Putin.[58]) During the period between 1987 and 1991, Yeltsin undoubtedly played a part in the radicalization of political reform. At the time many of his actions served the cause of democratization, at least in the short term. In the light of his record as president, it is much less clear that Yeltsin's electoral success was of longer-term benefit to the development of democracy in Russia.

On the second transformation, Gorbachev played a significant part in undermining the command economy, but without establishing a viable alternative. It was Yeltsin who embraced a form of capitalism more wholeheartedly, though unfortunately it turned out to be a capitalism closer to that imagined and condemned in old, unreconstructed Soviet propaganda than what was to be found elsewhere in Europe. Certainly, in many respects the system constructed in the first post-Soviet decade—whether characterized in terms of Hellman's "partial reform equilibrium"[59] or Ericson's analogy between the Russian economy at the beginning of a new millennium and medieval European feudalism (with a "parcelization of sovereignty" and "manors" and "principalities" exercising traditional authority and patterns of interaction within their respective domains, including vis-à-vis industrial enterprises)[60]—was still not a market economy. However, even if Gorbachev had taken the necessary first steps towards dismantling the Soviet economic system and was committed in principle to movement towards the market, Yeltsin's support for Gaidar's price liberalization and, subsequently, for remarkably speedy (and seriously flawed) privatization meant that he was the more thoroughgoing economic transformer of the two leaders.

The third and fourth transformations, in contrast, saw Yeltsin playing no part whatsoever and Gorbachev playing the decisive role. Even if the end of the Cold War is dated as late as 1990, with the unification of Germany, rather than linked to the dramatic change in Soviet foreign policy whose full dimensions were made clear in 1988 or to the end of communist regimes in Eastern Europe in 1989, all that took place before Yeltsin had an opportunity even to begin to be involved sporadically in the conduct of foreign policy. Yeltsin started to be taken somewhat more seriously as a foreign policy actor after the failed coup of August 1991 but was fully recognized as such only from January 1992, following the disappearance of the Soviet Union. By then, Gorbachev's acceptance of the end of communist rule in Eastern Europe (the fourth of the transformations) had not only ended the Cold War by removing any reason for it (and earned him the Nobel Peace

Prize) but, more dangerously for Gorbachev, had led to intensified pressures on him within the Soviet Union itself. Nations, especially in the Baltic republics, where independent statehood was widely desired but had for decades seemed a forlorn hope, suddenly saw that what had turned out to be possible for the Central European members of a now-defunct Warsaw Pact might be feasible also for Estonians, Latvians, and Lithuanians. Their intensified pressure on the all-union leadership and on Gorbachev personally naturally made their hard-line opponents increasingly agitated and restive and set the scene for the fifth of the transformations, the breakup of the Soviet Union.

The parts played by Gorbachev and Yeltsin in that transformation are less clear-cut, and the breakup itself was by no means so unambiguously positive a development as the move from an authoritarian to a pluralistic political system undoubtedly was. As in the other transformations, many political actors naturally played a part. In this particular instance, leaders within the Baltic states were in the vanguard of demands for independent statehood—not least Lithuania's Algirdas-Mikolas Brazauskas. Gorbachev's role, as suggested above, was largely an unintended consequence of, on the one hand, his domestic liberalization and democratization and, on the other, his transformation of Soviet foreign policy which had put an end to the "outer empire" and had established harmonious relations with former Western antagonists. Gorbachev had made clear to the East European Communist Party leaders from the earliest days of his general secretaryship that there would be no more Soviet military interventions to sustain them. Once this had become more public knowledge and, more specifically, after Soviet troops in Eastern Europe remained in their barracks as regimes fell around them, expectations were naturally raised among every nationality in the Soviet Union with a sense of grievance, of whom there were many.

Yet it is possible that a union treaty might have been voluntarily agreed to by a *majority* of the fifteen republics that made up the USSR had Yeltsin not adopted an increasingly maximalist stance and played the Russian card against the union. Once the leadership of Russia had abandoned the union as, in the shape of Yeltsin, it had come close to doing even before the putschists in August 1991 achieved the opposite of what they intended and gave an added stimulus to separatism, it was becoming clear even to those republic leaders who wished to preserve a union that the cause was lost. For Gorbachev throughout 1991, nothing—not even the deteriorating economic situation—was more important than the attempt to preserve some kind of union. Thus, his contribution to its breakup was a side effect of policies pursued for other ends, whereas Yeltsin contributed to it much more purposefully. That was not because it was a goal he desired per se, but for the simple reason that with no union there would be no Gorbachev. Still striving to be the undisputed number one, Yeltsin was ready to cede territory that had been part of a greater Russian state for centuries in pursuit of that end.

Where people stand on the breakup of the Soviet Union depends partly on where they sit. That it was a transformation, for better or worse, no one can deny. However, a majority of the successor states to the Soviet Union have authoritarian regimes—more authoritarian, indeed, than they were in the last years of the Soviet Union when democratizing developments in Moscow still had some impact on, for instance, the Central Asian republics or Belarus. With all the limitations of its hybrid polity, Russia is nevertheless probably closer to democracy than eleven of the successor states. Only Estonia, Latvia, and Lithuania are unambiguously more democratic. Thus, if much has gone wrong for Russians over the past fifteen or sixteen years, there is much that has also gone right. In terms of all manner of liberties, notwithstanding serious pressures on the most independent parts of the mass media which became more overt after Vladimir Putin succeeded Yeltsin, Russia is a far freer country than it was in all but the last few years of the Soviet Union.

The Gorbachevian optimism of 1988–1989, shared then by most of his fellow citizens and much of the outside world, has gone. But so have the illusions of Yeltsin and many of his Western admirers that he had established a working democracy and a market economy. (Whatever worries genuine democrats may have about Yeltsin's successor, it is at least to Putin's credit that he has introduced a new realism into the Kremlin.) Now that the days in power of the two septuagenarian leaders (Yeltsin was 70 in February 2001 and the much more vigorous Gorbachev reached that landmark just one month later) are behind them, it is clear that the highest of hopes which at different times each of them engendered have not been realized, but neither have the worst fears. Indeed, what occurred after Gorbachev came to power in 1985 far exceeded, on the various dimensions discussed in this chapter, the expectations of even the optimists among those who hoped for an easing of East-West tensions and a more tolerant and freer Russia. Amidst all the conflicting pulls and pushes of events, courageous and enlightened leadership in Moscow, with Gorbachev making the essential breakthrough, played the decisive and indispensable part in producing largely peaceful systemic change.

I am grateful for suggestions made by Tomila Lankina and the Carnegie readers.

Notes

1. See Mikhail Gorbachev, *Gorbachev on My Country and the World* (New York: Columbia University Press, 1999), esp. part 2, "The Union Could Have Been Preserved," pp. 83–167.

2. Aleksandr Korzhakov, *Boris Yel'tsin: Ot rassveta do zakata* (Moscow: Interbruk, 1997), p. 52.

3. See Leon Aron, *Boris Yeltsin: A Revolutionary Life* (London: HarperCollins, 2000), pp. 200–212; and Archie Brown, *The Gorbachev Factor* (Oxford: Oxford University Press, 1996), pp. 169–172.

4. Jack F. Matlock, Jr., *Autopsy on an Empire: The American Ambassador's Account of the Collapse of the Soviet Union* (New York: Random House, 1995), p. 210.

5. I have more to say on the foreign influences in *The Gorbachev Factor,* chapters 3 and 4, and in "Transnational Influences in the Transition from Communism," *Post-Soviet Affairs* 16, no. 2 (2000): 177–200.

6. It was, nevertheless, as late as May 1990 that Yeltsin overtook Gorbachev as the most popular political figure in Russia and the Soviet Union, according to VTsIOM, then as now the most reliable of the public opinion polling organizations in Russia.

7. See *Sovetskaya Rossiya,* 13 March 1988; *Pravda,* 5 April 1988; and M. S. Gorbachev, *Gody trudnykh resheniy* (Moscow: Alfa-Print, 1993), pp. 98–110.

8. Yegor Ligachev, *Inside Gorbachev's Kremlin* (New York: Pantheon, 1993), p. 90.

9. Vladimir Kryuchkov, *Lichnoe delo* (Moscow: Olimp, 1996), vol. 2, p. 360.

10. Brown, *The Gorbachev Factor,* pp. 145–146.

11. Joel Hellman, "Winners Take All: The Politics of Partial Reform in Postcommunist Transitions," *World Politics* 50 (January 1998): 203–234. See also Nodari Simonia, "Domestic Developments in Russia," in *Russia and Asia: The Emerging Security Agenda,* ed. Gennady Chufrin (Oxford: SIPRI with Oxford University Press, 1999), pp. 52–80; S. P. Peregudov, N. Yu. Lapina, and I. S. Semenenko, *Gruppy interesov v Rossiyskoe gosudarstvo* (Moscow: Editorial URSS, 1999), esp. pp. 289–302; Juliet Johnson, "Russia's Emerging Financial-Industrial Groups," *Post-Soviet Affairs* 13, no. 4 (1997): 333–365; and Archie Brown, "The Russian Crisis: Beginning of the End or End of the Beginning?" *Post-Soviet Affairs* 15, no. 1 (1999): 56-73.

12. See, e.g., Alena V. Ledeneva, *Russia's Economy of Favours: Blat, Networking and Informal Exchange* (Cambridge: Cambridge University Press, 1998), esp. chapter 6; A. V. Ledeneva and M. Kurkchiyan, eds., *Economic Crime in Russia* (The Hague and London: Kluwer Law International, 2000), esp. chapter 1; Natalia Dinello, "The Russian F-Connection: Finance, Firms, Friends, Families and Favorites," *Problems of Post-Communism* 46, no. 1 (1999): 24–33; and

Chrystia Freeland, *Sale of the Century: The Inside Story of the Second Russian Revolution* (London: Little, Brown, 2000).

13. Richard E. Ericson, "Is Russia in Transition to a Market Economy?" *Post-Soviet Affairs* 16, no. 1 (January-March 2000): 18–25.

14. Boris Yeltsin, *Midnight Diaries* (London: Weidenfeld & Nicolson, 2000), p. 96.

15. Gosplan was the State Planning Committee, and Gossnab the State Committee on Material-Technical Supplies. Those "State Committees" were in reality superministries with wide-ranging responsibilities. Also important in the Soviet economic policy-making process were the economic departments of the Central Committee of the Communist Party. Almost all of the latter were, however, abolished by Gorbachev as early as 1988.

16. Pavel Palazchenko, *My Years with Gorbachev and Shevardnadze* (University Park: Pennsylvania State University Press, 1997), p. 372.

17. Ibid.

18. George Shultz, *Turmoil and Triumph: My Years as Secretary of State* (New York: Macmillan, 1993), p. 1138.

19. Robert E. English, *Russia and the Idea of the West* (New York: Columbia University Press, 2000), p. 212.

20. Ibid. See also Matthew Evangelista, *Unarmed Forces: The Transnational Movement to End the Cold War* (Ithaca, N.Y.: Cornell University Press, 1999).

21. The latest remotely plausible date for the ending of the Cold War would be the unification of Germany in 1990. See Timothy Garton Ash, *In Europe's Name: Germany and the Divided Continent* (London: Jonathan Cape, 1993); and Philip Zelikow and Condoleezza Rice, *Germany Unified and Europe Transformed: A Study in Statecraft* (Cambridge: Harvard University Press, 1995).

22. Jacques Lévesques, *The Enigma of 1989: The USSR and the Liberation of Eastern Europe* (Berkeley and Los Angeles: University of California Press, 1997), p. 87.

23. Vadim Medvedev, *Raspad* (Moscow: Mezhdunarodnye otnosheniya, 1994). See also Medvedev, *Prozrenie, mif ili predatel'stvo? K voprosu ob ideologii perestroyki* (Moscow: Evraziya, 1998); A. S. Chernyaev, *Shest' let s Gorbachevym: Po dnevnikovym pomoshchnika* (Moscow: Kultura, 1993); and, for a more critical view of Gorbachev's conduct of foreign policy, V. M. Falin, *Bez skidok na obstoyatel'stva: politicheskie vospominaniya* (Moscow: Respublika, 1999).

24. Gorbachev, *On My Country and the World*, p. 206.

25. The International Department, it is worth noting, was itself a body that had harbored important "new thinkers" as well as traditionalists. It was from there that Anatoliy Chernyaev and Andrey Grachev, for example, came to work directly on Gorbachev's team.

26. Falin, *Bez skidok na obstoyatel'stva*, esp. pp. 447, 452, 453.

27. Author's interview with Chernyaev, 30 March 1992.

28. Anatoly Dobrynin, *In Confidence: Moscow's Ambassador to America's Six Cold War Presidents* (New York: Random House, 1995), p. 628.

29. For elaboration of this point, see Rogers Brubaker, *Nationalism Reframed: Nationhood and the National Question in the New Europe* (Cambridge: Cambridge University Press, 1996); Valerie Bunce, *Subversive Institutions: The Design and the Destruction of Socialism and the State* (Cambridge: Cambridge University Press, 1999); and Alfred Stepan, "Russian Federalism in Comparative Perspective," *Post-Soviet Affairs* 16, no. 2 (2000): 133–176.

30. Jerry Hough, *Democratization and Revolution in the USSR 1985-1991* (Washington, D.C.: Brookings Institution, 1997), p. 498.

31. On the Tbilisi killings, see Brown, *The Gorbachev Factor,* pp. 264–267.

32. For a defense of Gorbachev's policies in this sphere, see A. B. Veber, V. T. Loginov, G. S. Ostroumov, and A. S. Chernyaev, eds., *Soyuz mozhno bylo sokhranit': dokumenty i fakty o politike M.S. Gorbacheva po reformirovaniyu i sokhraneniyu mnogonatsional'nogo gosudarstva* (Moscow: Gorbachev Foundation, 1995). Cf. Vera Tolz and Iain Elliot, eds., *The Demise of the USSR: From Communism to Independence* (London: Macmillan, 1995).

33. Aron, *Boris Yeltsin,* p. 375.

34. Ibid., p. 377.

35. Alexander Dallin, "Causes of the Collapse of the USSR," *Post-Soviet Affairs* 8, no. 4 (1992): 279–302.

36. Ibid., 299.

37. Ibid.

38. Ibid.

39. Matthew Wyman's broad-ranging study of the findings of survey research in the last years of the Soviet era and early years of post-Soviet Russia show that there was only a very brief period of time when a general reluctance on the part of the Soviet population to endorse the use of force went so far as for a majority of Russians to approve of the breakup of the Soviet Union. Apart from this fleeting moment at the end of 1991, a majority of Russians (before then) wished to preserve the union and (after its demise) regretted the loss of the Soviet state. See Wyman, *Public Opinion in Postcommunist Russia* (Basingstoke and London: Macmillan, 1997), esp. pp. 172–173.

40. Aron, *Boris Yeltsin,* p. 736.

41. See Yu. A. Baturin, A. L. Il'in, V. F. Kadatskiy, V. V. Kostikov, M. A. Krasnov, A. Ya. Livshitz, K. V. Nikiforov, L. G. Pikhoya, and G. A. Satarov, *Epokha Yel'tsina* (Moscow: Vagrius, 2001), p. 226. Although the authors, all of whom worked closely with the Russian president, are loyal to Yeltsin and display a definite bias against Gorbachev—relying, for example, on a tendentiously selective reading of the self-justificatory accounts of the putschists when discussing Gorbachev's position during the August 1991 coup against him—their recently published substantial volume is useful inasmuch as it provides new, documentary material on some of the workings of Yeltsin's inner circle in post-Soviet Russia.

42. Ibid.

43. Ibid.

44. On total loyalty to him as Yeltsin's *sine qua non,* see, for example, Yevgeniy Primakov, *Gody v bol'shoy politike,* p. 223; Sergey Filatov, *Sovershenno nesekretno* (Moscow: Vagrius, 2000), p. 166; and Oleg Poptsov, *Khronika vremen "Tsarya Borisa"* (Moscow: "Sovershenno Sekretno," 1996), pp. 104, 106.

45. See the valuable article by George Breslauer focusing on the patriarchal aspect of Yeltsin's political style, "Boris Yel'tsin as Patriarch," *Post-Soviet Affairs* 15, no. 2 (1999): 186–200, esp. 197.

46. V. M. Sukhodrev, *Yazyk moy—arut moy: Ot Khrushcheva do Gorbacheva* (Moscow: Olimp, 1999), p. 423; and Chernyaev, *Shest' let s Gorbachevym,* p. 317.

47. Shakhnazarov, for long a closet social democrat within the Central Committee apparatus, in post-Soviet Russia headed the Center for Global Programs of the Gorbachev Founda-

tion. He died suddenly on May 15, 2001, aged 76. For obituaries, see *The Times* (London), 21 May 2001, p. 17; and *Literaturnaya gazeta*, no. 21, 23–29 May 2001, p. 2.

48. Korzhakov, *Boris Yel'tsin: ot rassveta do zakata*, p. 118.

49. Raisa Gorbacheva, in a conversation I had with her on 28 October 1996, confirmed that she had been "categorically against" her husband standing in the 1996 presidential election.

50. Yegor Gaidar, *Dni porazheniy i pobed* (Moscow: Vagrius, 1997), p. 106.

51. Ibid.

52. Two books that complement each other admirably and illustrate that point very convincingly are Eugene Huskey's *Presidential Power in Russia* (Armonk and London: M. E. Sharpe, 1999), and Lilia Shevtsova's *Yeltsin's Russia: Myths and Reality* (Washington, D.C.: Carnegie Endowment for International Peace, 1999).

53. See Yeltsin, *Midnight Diaries,* pp. 23–27; and Peter Reddaway, "Will Putin be Able to Consolidate Power?" *Post-Soviet Affairs* 17, no. 1 (2001): 23–44, at 26.

54. Brezhnev said to a member of the Politburo of the Communist Party of Czechoslovakia, Bohumil Šimon, who led a delegation to Moscow in November 1968: "If I hadn't voted in the politburo for military intervention, what would have happened? You almost certainly would not be sitting here. And I probably wouldn't be sitting here either." See Zdeněk Mlynář, *Night Frost in Prague: The End of Humane Socialism* (London: Hurst, 1980), p. 163.

55. Gaidar, *Dni porazheniy i pobed,* p. 141.

56. Even Yeltsin, in his earliest volume of memoirs, wrote of Gorbachev: "What he has achieved will, of course, go down in the history of mankind. I do not like high-sounding phrases; yet everything that Gorbachev has initiated deserves such praise. He could have gone on existing just as Brezhnev and Chernenko existed before him. I estimate that the country's natural resources and the people's patience would have lasted for the length of his lifetime, long enough for him to have lived out the well-fed and happy life of the leader of a totalitarian state. He could have draped himself with orders and medals, the people would have hymned him in verse and song, which is always very enjoyable. Yet Gorbachev chose to go quite another way." Boris Yeltsin, *Against the Grain: An Autobiography* (London: Jonathan Cape, 1990), p. 113.

57. See Brown, *The Gorbachev Factor,* esp. pp. 309–315.

58. Archie Brown, ed., *Contemporary Russian Politics: A Reader* (Oxford: Oxford University Press, 2001), esp. section 12, pp. 513–568.

59. Hellman, "Winners Take All."

60. Ericson, "Is Russia in Transition to a Market Economy?" esp. pp. 23–24.

3

Evaluating Gorbachev and Yeltsin as Leaders

George W. Breslauer

Ten years after the collapse of the USSR, we can look back on the administrations of four men whose names and faces dominated the public representation of Soviet and post-Soviet-Russian politics for the last 48 years: Nikita Khrushchev, Leonid Brezhnev, Mikhail Gorbachev, and Boris Yeltsin. These men shared the challenge of dealing with the inherited dysfunctions or legacy of the post-Stalinist Soviet political system. But the four differed in their conceptions of what to do about those dysfunctions. Khrushchev tried to *reform* the system; Brezhnev tried to *consolidate and adapt* it; Gorbachev attempted to *transform* it into a socialist democracy; and Yeltsin sought ultimately to *destroy and replace it.* The differences in their objectives in turn dictated differences in the approaches they adopted to leadership. This chapter focuses on the leadership provided by Gorbachev and Yeltsin during 1985–2000. The purpose is to render a preliminary evaluation of the quality of their leadership.

On Leadership Evaluation

In both journalism and academic scholarship, leadership evaluation takes place all the time—but usually without reflection on the standards being applied. Consequently, different standards may be applied to the same leader by different observers, leading to divergent bottom-line evaluations. I begin, therefore, by setting standards for judging Gorbachev and Yeltsin as leaders.

One standard is purely normative, with the norms determined by the observer: do I agree or disagree with the values and goals being pursued by the leader? If I agree with those values and goals, I call him or her "great." If I dislike those values and goals, he or she cannot qualify as "great." A normative approach might also focus on the results of a leader's policies. If I approve of those results, I render a positive evaluation; if I disagree, my judgment will be negative. (As Hoffmann puts it, "a man who is a hero to my neighbor may be a calamity to me."[1]) More often than not, a normative approach to evaluation will conflate intentions and results, treating the latter as a product of the former.

For example, those who disliked what Gorbachev stood for often brought great passion to their negative evaluations, while those who liked what he was doing often displayed "Gorbymania." *Time* magazine might proclaim Gorbachev its "Man of the Decade," even as Soviet reactionaries, on one side of the spectrum, were damning his Westernization of the country and Soviet free-marketeers, on the other side of the spectrum, were damning his stubborn retention of a commitment to the "socialist idea." People at both ends of the Soviet political spectrum expressed dismay that Gorbachev came eventually to be so much admired abroad, yet so little admired at home. When the debate over a leader's "performance" hinges largely on acceptance or rejection of the values he or she pursued or realized, the debate need not detain us long. It is not amenable to resolution through the marshaling of evidence. The dispute may detour into a philosophical discussion of the relative merits of different values, but that is a different task than evaluating leadership per se.

While a purely normative approach is too constricting, we still need a standard by which to judge a leader's performance. Hence, a second approach to leadership evaluation hinges principally on judgments about *effectiveness*. Of course, effectiveness can only be determined relative to a set of goals: effective at achieving *what*? Hence, goals and values must be part of the equation. Taking as our standard the *observer's* values does not get us very far if these differ from the values of the leader in question. It does not make sense to evaluate leaders' effectiveness in achieving goals they were not pursuing. Hence, performance evaluation that is based on a standard of effectiveness must take *the leader's* goals and values as the standard and judge his or her effectiveness in advancing those goals. How well did Gorbachev and Yeltsin perform as leaders in pursuit of the goals they embraced?

This approach need not entail approval of the leader's goals. An observer who disagrees with the leader's goals may nonetheless begrudgingly concede that he or she was highly effective in achieving them. Conversely, an observer who agrees with the goals may sadly concede that the leader proved ineffective in achieving them. And to fill out the possibilities: an observer may disagree with the goals and celebrate the leader's ineffectiveness in pursuing them. Or the observer may agree with the goals and celebrate the leader's effectiveness in achieving them.

Effectiveness typically comes at a price. Leaders may achieve their goals at high or low cost to other values. Stalin is an obvious case in point. He built up the military and industrial strength of the country at enormous human and economic cost. Leadership evaluation will therefore hinge on the magnitude of the cost associated with goal-attainment. Leaders who achieve their goals at low cost to collateral values may be deemed more effective than those who impose a very high price for goal-attainment.

It does not follow, however, that observers will dub such leaders "great." Such characterizations hinge more on the observer's values. If we deeply cherish the values sacrificed for the sake of goal-attainment—such as the millions of human lives sacrificed by Stalin—we may concede that Stalin was an effective but dastardly leader who attained his goals at an *unacceptable* price. To bring this point closer to the present, one could concede that Boris Yeltsin was effective in sustaining the territorial unity of the Russian Federation, but condemn him for the price he was willing to pay toward this end in prosecuting two wars in Chechnya. Or, with a similar logic, one could give Gorbachev high marks for attaining his goals of liberalization and democratization, but condemn him for proving willing to do so at the expense of the disintegration of the USSR.

It is not surprising that those who condemn Yeltsin's leadership most vociferously also view the social and human costs of his policies as huge; and they argue as well that those costs—such as the decline in the life-expectancy of Russian men and women—were direct products of his policies, that is, costs that would not have been borne in the absence of his policies.[2] Similarly, those who most vociferously condemn Gorbachev's leadership tend to be those who most valued the Soviet system, the USSR, and/or the country's global power status and attribute direct causal responsibility to Gorbachev for the loss of those values.[3] Expressed in this way, the cost of goal-attainment is acceptable or unacceptable according to the observer's scale of values. This is an appropriate standard for an evaluative exercise, which cannot escape some normative component. But it is not amenable to resolution through the marshaling of evidence. Hence, a social-scientific approach to leadership evaluation will logically veer toward another set of issues: what was the alternative? How effective would alternative strategies have been for attaining the goals at a lower price?

The Inescapability of Counterfactual Reasoning

Leaders and their supporters often defend themselves against criticism of the costs of their policies by invoking an image of intractable constraints. The implication is that advancement or defense of cherished values could not have been accomplished by other means. That is a counterfactual claim. Thus, Vyacheslav Molotov, a leading Politburo member under Stalin, referred to the human and economic cost of Stalinist policies as "regrettable necessities." Hard-line Stalinists in many countries deflected criticism of the costs of Stalinism by arguing that "you cannot make an omelette without breaking eggs."[4] Gorbachev and his supporters tried to parry criticism from party conservatives by arguing that "there is no alternative" and that "there is no other way" (*inogo nye dano*). Defenders of Yeltsin's policies in Chechnya argued that even Abraham Lincoln had to prosecute an enormously costly civil war in order to hold the United States together. Defenders of Yeltsin's neoliberal macroeconomic policies frequently argued that alternatives to their preferred policies would not work.

In all these cases, the counterfactual is usually buttressed by a theoretical claim. Stalin invoked a theory of state-building, nation-building, and economic development in a hostile international environment that seemed to narrow drastically the set of policies claimed to be effective in such a setting. Gorbachev's defenders suggested that only a policy that shattered the immunity of the party-state elite could overcome the systemic stagnation that had beset the ancien regime. Yeltsin's defenders claimed that, even in democratic systems, force is required to prevent armed secession. Yeltsin's neoliberal advisers similarly argued that "shock therapy" constituted the only viable strategy for making the transition from a command economy to a market economy.

Both critics and defenders of Gorbachev and Yeltsin often join the argument, not on theoretical grounds, but on the basis of an empirical estimation of the intellectual availability, political feasibility, and practicability of alternative policies in the given historical context. Thus, when people criticize Gorbachev for not having pushed through a Chinese-style economic reform, and for not having adopted radical price reform early in his tenure,[5] his defenders claim that it was far from clear that such policies would have worked in the USSR as they did in China and equally unclear that price liberalization would have been compatible with political stability.[6] When Yeltsin is condemned for adopting neoliberal policies in January 1992,[7] his defenders argue that, in the concrete economic circumstances of the time, alternative policies would have resulted either in financial and economic collapse or in the kind of prolonged depression that marked the unreformed Ukrainian economy.[8] And when Yeltsin is criticized for not being more accommodating to the political opposition in the Supreme Soviet and Duma,[9] his defenders argue or imply that the opposition was more powerful and more reactionary in orientation than Yeltsin's critics allow. They argue that the opposition had both the strength and the inclination to win power and to restore some variant of the old regime—hence, that the alternative, by this observer's scale of values, would have been worse.[10]

In short, evaluation of leaders' effectiveness in attaining their goals at a proportionate price hinges also on one's image of the strength of the constraints facing them at the time. If the constraints were onerous, we would normally expect less accomplishment than if the constraints were easy to overcome. Leaders who manage to stretch (but not obliterate) the social constraints in their environment, and thereby initiate substantial movement at an acceptable cost, are typically deemed both effective and impressive. By contrast, leaders who are defeated by those constraints may be deemed ineffective but doomed to failure, if the constraints are perceived to have been immutable; or they may be judged ineffective and incompetent, if they failed to seize the opportunities available. And if leaders accomplish much, but in a context in which the constraints were few and malleable, they may be judged to have been effective but unimpressive ("anybody could have done it").

Thus, leadership cannot be evaluated without some conception of its flip side: opportunity. If the challenge was so great as to be impossible to achieve, then, by definition, no amount of brilliance could have overcome the constraints. Under such circumstances, there was no opportunity to exploit. On the other hand, if the challenge was a simple one, or if existing social and political forces would have pushed through the observed changes in any case, then the leader can hardly be credited with having "made history."

Notice that making these judgments requires us to think in counterfactual terms. We may gather a large amount of evidence regarding the nature of the constraints, the strength of social forces, and the like. But without trying to imagine how these constraints and forces would have evolved *in the absence of the leader in question,* or in the presence of either a stronger or weaker leader, we cannot specify either the magnitude of the opportunity or the indispensability of a given leader for exploiting it. Since other leaders were not in power, and other approaches to getting things done were not attempted, we cannot test with high confidence the size of the opportunity that was available. The difficulty in addressing the "might have beens" of history has led many historians to disparage counterfactual thought experiments as little more than fruitless speculation or parlor games.[11]

But if one tosses out counterfactual reasoning, one must also toss out leadership evaluation. Methodologically, a convincing exercise in leadership evaluation must interweave counterfactual reasoning with traditional methods of analysis and explanation. It must combine disciplined speculation about available alternatives with analysis of the strength of constraints and efforts to specify the causes of outcomes. Thus, leadership evaluation must seek to determine how much causal responsibility to assign to the exercise of leadership for the outcomes observed. And it must ask whether hypothetical alternatives were indeed available. It must analyze the magnitude of the task, the magnitude and mutability of the constraints on change, and the magnitude of the divergence from the traditional, and currently available, skills and mentality required to carry out the task in the face of those constraints. Ultimately, it must address such questions as to what extent was the individual's repertoire of leadership skills, and the leadership strategy he or she adopted, a necessary (albeit not sufficient) condition for achieving the results observable during his or her years in power? How different would things have been had this individual not been in power? Could other individuals who were available at the time have accomplished as much as, or more than, this leader did? How powerful were the political constraints on available choices? Could these leaders have gotten away with more than they dared to attempt? Or would they have been forced from power—or at least frustrated—had they tried?

Given all these uncertainties, we might be tempted to abandon the task of leadership evaluation—or to consign it to journalistic exercises in special issues of popular magazines.[12] That would be unwise. Historians and social scientists do not abandon their craft because the evidence is inconclusive; they seek to make the best of what they have, and to present their conclusions as tentative and always subject to future revision. The same goes for counterfactual speculation, which is not as different from historical explanation, methodologically and epistemologically, as many historians assume.[13] Moreover, no matter how indeterminate the exercise, people will go on evaluating leaders, for better or for worse, and their evaluations of leaders-in-power will sometimes feed back into the political process. How scholars, politicians, and journalists evaluate current or historical leaders can influence present-day politics. Indeed, with respect to current leaders being evaluated while in office, it can become part of the social constraints they face and can influence the opportunities they enjoy—and thereby affect their prospects of eventually succeeding or failing! Hence, to abandon leadership evaluation because of its inconclusiveness or indeterminacy is to abandon scholarship. And eschewing it because of its normative components and possible political impact is an unnecessary act of scholarly abdication.

Gorbachev and Yeltsin were unmistakably "event-making men."[14] Both of them began as reformers of the system and then sought to transform or replace it, though they chose very different strategies for achieving their goals. Both of them faced huge constraints at home and abroad. Both of them were unique figures within elite circles. It is difficult to imagine other leaders at the time who would have made an analogous degree of difference. In evaluating Gorbachev's and Yeltsin's effectiveness as leaders, then, we must address the extent to which they achieved their stated goals and the price they proved willing to pay to do so.

Gorbachev as a Transformational Leader

Transformational leadership is a process of what Schumpeter called "creative destruction": dismantling of the old system in a way that simultaneously creates the foundations for a new system.[15] This is a tall order for the most talented of leaders. When the point of departure is a monopolistic Leninist system, a transformational leader must: 1) create and legitimize autonomous public arenas; 2) disperse social, economic, political, and informational resources into those arenas; 3) construct new institutions for coordination of decentralized social exchange and integration of the new social order; and 4) plant the seeds of a new political-economic culture that is consonant with the new social order. Thus, he or she must destroy the structures and culture of the old order, put new structures in their place, and help articulate a new culture.

That, in any case, is the ideal. Rare is the leader who is able to succeed in both system-destruction and system-building. Gorbachev and Yeltsin are two men who tried to be successful on both counts. We may therefore analyze and compare their efforts, both to assess the effectiveness of their performance as transformational leaders and to specify the factors that influenced their choices.

Baselines for Evaluation

Among observers who shared his goal of transforming the communist system, those who most approve of Gorbachev's record as leader emphasize the extent to which he broke down the ancien regime. Among the same set of observers, those who most disparage Gorbachev's record focus instead on the extent to which he fell short of building the new system he envisaged. Neither of these approaches is wholly satisfying; nor is a combination of the two. They are both linear and rote comparisons of outcomes with baselines. But they are useful starting points toward a more complex analysis.

If the past is our baseline, and if we postpone the problem of determining Gorbachev's distinctive contribution to the outcome, it is easy to sum up what changed under Gorbachev. We witnessed:

1. desacralization of the Brezhnevite political-economic order in the eyes of the mass public, including the official principles and mindset that underpinned it: the leading role of the Communist Party; the "community of peoples"; the Planned Economy; pride in the system's achievements; optimism about state socialism's potential; commitment to "class struggle" abroad; and a national-security phobia that justified a repressive, militarized regime;

2. a sharp reduction in the power of constituencies that were pillars of the Brezhnevite political order: party officials, ministers, and the military, in particular;

3. legitimation in principle of movement in the direction of a market-driven economic order, a multiparty system, and the transformation of a unitary state into a democratic-federal state;

4. changes in politics and structure that: greatly decentralized political initiative; created more open and competitive public-political arenas, including parliaments based on competitive, secret-ballot elections; all but disenfranchised the *nomenklatura*; and swept radical majorities into power in the governmental councils of major cities;

5. dismantling of much of the command economy and the emergence of a nascent private sector ("cooperatives");

6. introduction of civil liberties with respect to dissent, emigration, the media, travel, religion, and association;

7. a vast opening of the country to Western political, cultural, and economic influences;

8. elimination of Soviet control over Eastern Europe, reduction of Soviet military capabilities, retrenchment in Third World policy, and withdrawal of Soviet troops from Afghanistan; and

9. changes in foreign policy that brought an end to the Cold War.

Historically, only revolutions from below have accomplished more in a shorter period of time. And revolutions from below have never been marked by the scant violence that Gorbachev's revolution entailed.

Using the same methodology, however, one could specify how much had not changed during the Gorbachev era, or had changed for the worse by a short-term humanitarian standard:

1. a doleful consumer situation that, in 1990–1991, was worse that it had been in 1985;

2. an economy that was experiencing accelerating negative growth of national income, ridden by a huge budgetary deficit and monetary overhang, and suffering from potentially explosive repressed inflation;

3. economic disorganization, lack of coordination, and massive corruption resulting from destruction of the institutions of a command economy without the construction of institutions of a market economy;

4. widespread intercommunal violence in the southern republics of the USSR;

5. disintegration of the unitary state, along with centrifugal pressures that left the country on the verge of separatism by half the republics in the union;

6. a sharp increase in the incidence of violent crime throughout the country; and

7. failure to induce the rich democracies to underwrite the Soviet economic transition.

Were the changes between 1985 and 1991 on balance positive or negative? This is a normative judgment. The answer depends on the relative weights placed on the values in question. Clearly, one glance at these lists indicates that things worsened with respect to the economic situation and the cohesion of the USSR as an entity, while things improved in the areas of political freedom, cultural openness, and East-West relations, with "improvement" measured according to Gorbachev's professed scale of values.[16]

Another approach would take as its baseline not the past but the vision of a future new order. The easy variant of this approach is simply to measure the shortfall between Soviet reality in mid-1991 and Gorbachev's vision of a stable, social(ist)-democratic polity, integrated into Western institutions and treated internationally as a great power, a tolerable federation or confederation, and a prospectively flourishing mixed economy, based on a combination of private, collective, and state ownership.[17] By this standard, Gorbachev surely fell short as a transformational leader. He did not succeed in steering an evolutionary transition from the Soviet system to a system based on these ordering principles. Instead, the house collapsed upon him and he was ousted from office.

Gorbachev: An Event-Making Man?

If we treat the list of positive changes between 1985 and 1991 as the basis for a positive evaluation of Gorbachev as leader, we assume that he himself was causally responsible for the changes. That would be too generous a judgment, for we know that, after 1989, many outcomes were products of forces over which he had little control. But we can still ask whether, on balance, Gorbachev was an "event-making man" whose uncommon personal traits led to outcomes that would not have taken place in the absence of the leadership he provided. In this exercise, the issue is not normative but causal. It does not matter whether we approve or disapprove of the outcomes, only whether we believe that Gorbachev was responsible for bringing them about. By this standard, Gorbachev was indeed an event-making man.

Changes in social structure during the post-Stalin decades are insufficient to explain the policy changes that took place during 1985–1989, though a focus on societal initiatives probably does explain much of what happened in 1990–1991. The social forces supportive of perestroika, glasnost, democratization, and "new thinking" in foreign policy encouraged and facilitated Gorbachev's policies. Indeed, they were probably necessary conditions for the new policies to be enacted, implemented, and sustained. It is difficult, for example, to imagine Gorbachev having accomplished as much as he did, had he been leading the Soviet Union in 1955 rather than 1985. But the changes that had taken place in Soviet society, while providing a support base for Gorbachev to activate, were not sufficient to force policy makers to enact the policies Gorbachev sponsored. The relationship between social forces and sociopolitical change was heavily dependent on political leadership.

Gorbachev exercised active, determined leadership in the years following his consolidation of power. He intervened repeatedly to let the glasnost genie out of the bottle, to encourage the public to criticize the bureaucrats, to hold off the forces of backlash, to recall Andrey Sakharov from exile, to release political prisoners, and to force through a democratization program that began the process of transferring power from the party to the soviets. Gorbachev made the decisions that led to steadily expanding civil liberties of all sorts. Gorbachev also made the doctrinal pronouncements that encouraged or tolerated *public* desacralization of the Brezhnevite order. This desacralization induced societal activists to believe that fundamental change was not only desirable and necessary (which many of them had probably believed already), but *possible* as well. And Gorbachev's pronouncements had the simultaneous effect of discouraging recalcitrant bureaucrats from thinking that they could hold back the tide.

Gorbachev took the lead on matters of foreign policy, often surprising his domestic political audiences with announcements of Soviet concessions on nuclear and conventional arms control, making the fundamental decision to cut losses in Afghanistan, and later pulling the rug from under conservative East European elites by withdrawing the Soviet guarantee of protection against revolutionary forces. Gorbachev articulated a vision of a post-Cold War world, Soviet integration into the European cultural, political, and economic orders, and demilitarization of foreign policy that became the bases for both planning and legitimizing his turnabouts in domestic and foreign policy. Gorbachev decided to turn on the faucet of emigration once again and to allow Soviet citizens to travel to the West more freely.

To be sure, once sufficiently emboldened and organized, social forces pushed to radicalize Gorbachev's policies more quickly and more fully than he was comfortable with at the time. By late 1989, it is fair to say, Gorbachev had become a leader who was frequently reacting to degrees of radicalization he had not anticipated, desired, or controlled. These included the political resurrection of Boris Yeltsin; the mass demonstrations organized by "Democratic Russia"; the Baltic, Ukrainian, and Transcaucasian independence movements; intercommunal violence in the southern republics; certain activities of the Inter-Regional Group within the Congress of People's Deputies; coal miners' strikes in Siberia, Ukraine, and the Far East; and demands for abrogation of the "leading role of the party" in both the Soviet Union and Eastern Europe.

But in the face of this society-driven radicalization, Gorbachev had a choice. He could have allied with conservatives to "draw the line" and enforce strict limits. Instead, until his so-called "swing to the right" in late 1990, and with the exception of his response to intercommunal violence in the south, he typically made a virtue of necessity. He resisted the temptation to use force, often allying with more radical forces, using tactical surprise to further consolidate his power at the top, and purging or holding at bay those who would have preferred to use such radicalization as justification for reversing or halting the reform process. Thus, in 1989–1990, Gorbachev was more reactive than initiatory, but was still event-making in his ability to prevent the use of state-directed violence against the radicalizing tide. (A tragic exception occurred in Tbilisi in April 1989.[18]) When he lost his nerve and allied with more conservative forces in late 1990, he was no longer event-making at all, and actually inadvertently created the conditions for both the bloodshed in Vilnius and Riga (January 1991) and the coup of August 1991.

The event-making man not only makes a difference but does so because of his exceptional personal qualities. On this score, the evidence seems to be conclusive. Even those who criticize Gorbachev for the limits of his flexibility in his last years in power acknowledge that he was an unusual member of the Chernenko-led Politburo. No member of that Politburo has been portrayed as capable of seizing the initiative on sociopolitical and international issues the way Gorbachev eventually did. Gorbachev's intellectual capacity and flexibility, his powers of argumentation, his serenity in the midst of social turmoil, his faith that turbulence will "smooth out" in the long run,[19] his "sustained, single-minded motivation . . . an irrepressible optimism,"[20] his energy, determination, and tactical political skill,[21] and his capacity for learning on the job[22] have been noted by observers and interlocutors alike. By previous Soviet standards, as well as by comparative international standards, he stands out as a man of unusual leadership capacity. Had Gorbachev not been chosen general secretary after Chernenko's death, destruction of the Brezhnevite political order, the creation and nurturing of new democratic institutions and practices, and the radical concessionary turn in Soviet foreign policy would not have taken place as they did—or at all—in the 1980s.

Yeltsin as System-Destroyer

Boris Yeltsin sought to shake things up during his tenure as first secretary of the Moscow city party organization (1985–1987). But his semi-public critique of Ligachev in 1987 for going too slow on perestroika, and of Gorbachev for allegedly lapsing into complacency, led to his purge from both the secretaryship and the Politburo. Thereafter, by about 1989–1990, he had transformed himself into an anti-communist system-destroyer. His goal came to be to destroy the communist system along with all those features that Gorbachev hoped to preserve in the name of "socialism" and "Soviet civilization." Then, on the ruins of that system, Yeltsin proposed to build a new one on the territory of Russia, which he depicted as a "market democracy." This was the challenge he embraced during 1991–1999. These two phases of Yeltsin's political leadership may be subjected to separate evaluation.

During 1988–1991, Boris Yeltsin established himself as the hero of the anti-communist opposition to Soviet rule. After his overwhelming electoral victories of March 1989 and June 1991, followed by his facing down of the coup plotters in August 1991, his authority at home and abroad had become legendary. He had evolved into a charismatic leader of almost mythic proportions, especially among those who had assumed that the Soviet and communist control structures were unassailable. Thus, as an oppositional leader, Yeltsin is likely to go down in history as a uniquely courageous and effective figure who managed to prevail against seemingly overwhelming odds. His "resurrection" after being purged by the Communist Party apparatus in 1987 was a product of extraordinary political will, intuition, and an uncanny ability to sense and shape the mood of the masses. Moreover, his success during 1990–1991 in decoupling the concept of "Russian" from that of "Soviet" was both intellectually and politically inspired (given his goals), as was his insistence in March 1991 that Russia choose a president by popular election for the first time in its thousand-year history. Yeltsin was a revolutionary hero who achieved what he did through his extraordinary personal traits. Controversy is likely to be based largely on normative grounds. Those who approve of Yeltsin's role in destroying the communist and Soviet systems acclaim his leadership in this period, while those who disapprove of these ends censure him accordingly. But neither side would contest the observation, which is value-neutral, that Yeltsin was, in this leadership role, an "event-making man."[23]

Nothing that has happened since then is likely to alter this evaluation. Yeltsin's oppositional role of the 1980s—like Churchill's wartime leadership of Great Britain—can be judged independently of later events. It is an accomplished feat, capable of being assessed on its own terms.

When Yeltsin came to be president of independent Russia, communist ideology and organization had largely been destroyed. The constraints on progress were no longer products of the entrenchment of formal organizations and doctrines so much as their opposite: the fragmentation of governmental institutions; conflicting political jurisdictions within the inherited polity; disorganization of the economy and impending collapse of government finances; widespread disorientation and anxiety stemming from the collapse of the USSR; and the absence of an accepted worldview around which to rally the population, now that Gorbachev's "socialist choice" had been discredited. Yeltsin's agenda therefore had to focus on tasks of *construction*: state-building; nation-building; building a new economic and political order; forging a new international role for newly independent Russia; and defining an alternative worldview to justify the new institutions and policies. The tasks were both ideational and organizational, but in a context quite the opposite of what Gorbachev had faced when he first came to power. Once Yeltsin had finished administering the *coup de grace* to communist ideology and organization during 1989–1991, and to the USSR during 1991, he was faced with the challenge of creating new bases of order to put in their place.

In his capacity as president of Russia, Yeltsin sought to play three historic roles: 1) *founder* of a new state and nation; 2) *guarantor* of nascent democratic institutions, of processes of Westernization and privatization, and of the territorial integrity of the Russian state, against anarchy, secession, communist restoration, and/or xenophobic reaction; and 3) *integrator* of Russia into Western international organizations. Gorbachev had sought to transform an existing system into something qualitatively different by peaceful, evolutionary means. Yeltsin sought to abolish that system by nonviolent but revolutionary means and then to construct an alternative. How effective was he in building that alternative? How well did he play the roles of founder, guarantor, and integrator? And what price was he willing to pay toward those ends?

Yeltsin as System-Builder

Yeltsin was formulating policy in late-1991 under conditions vastly different from those in which Gorbachev found himself in 1985–1986. All the two had in common as they began their respective stages of ascendancy within the leadership was a belief that things could not be allowed to continue in the old way. To Yeltsin, this meant that drift and delay were not viable options, that hard choices could not be avoided or finessed, and that institutional fragmentation and economic decline could not be stopped without harsh measures. And he did indeed articulate a vision of an alternative system and an alternative strategy for reaching it: the neoliberal strategy preached to him by both international and domestic advocates and the vision of integration into a "normal," "civilized," Western international society.

In international affairs, in relations with the "Near Abroad," and with respect to Russian nation-building, Yeltsin was most successful in combining creativity with destruction, in balancing transformation with identity and stability, and in neutralizing the forces of reaction. In a difficult international and internal-political context, he managed to sell a combination of liberal-internationalism and realpolitik that flexed Russia's muscles while acknowledging Russia's weakness and seeking new associations abroad to offset it. In a difficult internal-political context, Yeltsin managed to advocate a combination of patriotism, ethnic pride, and liberal nationalism that rejected the extreme alternatives being offered by the "red-brown" coalition. In all these realms as well, he fostered the creation of institutions that could sustain a liberal orientation over the long term. Thus, his successes were both organizational and cultural—and held promise of sustainability.

But with respect to state-building and economic transformation, Yeltsin was much less effective. He may be credited with making the best of an unraveling economic situation in late 1991, when few alternative strategies appeared to be credible, though even this is a highly controversial claim.[24] And he may be credited with sustaining democratic processes and instituting a new constitutional framework through the sheer force of his will, at a time when the alternative appeared to be either reaction or gridlock. But it is in these realms that Yeltsin proved least able: 1) to engage in *creative destruction*; 2) to transform cultural and political attitudes toward belief in the new order; and 3) to create a climate, institutions, and processes for sustaining the transformation in the long term. Instead, by failing to create the organizational infrastructure of a market economy and democratic state, and by tolerating the de facto creation of a corrupt state and re-monopolized market that bore much resemblance to the Soviet system they had replaced, Yeltsin put at risk his entire project. By the time of his retirement, the market-democratic project was treated skeptically, if not with hostility, by much of the population, and nationalistic attitudes were on the rise that could lead eventually to a reversal even of the liberal successes in nation-building, relations with the Near Abroad, and East-West international relations.

That said, it is worth bearing in mind that the challenges of state-building and economic transformation required Yeltsin to overcome far more resilient obstacles and constraints than those he dealt with in the realms of foreign policy and symbolic politics. It is much easier to strike a deal with a foreign leader than to effect a permanent change in the culture and process of public administration. It is easier to speak publicly about the need for tolerance in interethnic relations than to deliver material satisfaction to the populace. It is also easier to deliver quick results in some realms than in others. Troop withdrawals from the Baltic states are easier and quicker to implement than is creation of the operating institutions of a regulatory state. Proper functioning of the "rule of law" requires both organizational and cultural change, both of which require a good deal of time and effort.

Moreover, Yeltsin was faced in these domestic realms with far more political and administrative constraints than in foreign policy. Unlike Gorbachev, he did not have a large apparatus of officials to process information and to whom he could delegate subtasks. He had to construct a "presidential administration" on the fly in 1991–1992 and himself was rapidly overloaded with decision-making responsibility. Then too, the opposition he faced from the Supreme Soviet in 1992–1993 would have impeded any efforts he might have launched to construct a rule of law in Russia. In short, any leader put in the situation Yeltsin was in at the end of 1991 would have faced a daunting array of constraints on his ability to implement a coherent, effective, and far-reaching strategy of state-building and economic transformation.

Yeltsin's failure to construct a robust organizational infrastructure happened to concern the most difficult problems for a president to overcome in a short period of time. Some presidents—notably, FDR and Charles de Gaulle—were up to the challenge, building organizations that would ultimately become the sinews of the U.S. and French regulatory states. Yeltsin was not up to the challenge, but he was also starting from a considerably more dire set of circumstances than either Roosevelt or de Gaulle faced. Moreover, both Gorbachev and Yeltsin failed on this score. Gorbachev was successful in building new political institutions for a democratized system, but not in building new economic institutions for a marketized, or post-command, economy or the institutions of a stable federalism. Both men appreciated the need to put an end to the command economy, but neither of them understood the institutional requirements for decentralizing economic administration.

Nonetheless, all of Yeltsin's accomplishments were real, and if Gorbachev is to be praised for "successfully" following a concessionary foreign policy, then Yeltsin can hardly be blamed for having done much of the same vis-à-vis both the rich democracies and many states in the Near Abroad. Similarly, if Gorbachev can be praised for breaking the political-psychological bonds of Leninist doctrine, then Yeltsin must be praised for his own contribution to cultural change: that is, his touting of a secular and tolerant definition of Russian citizenship and nationhood. If Gorbachev is to be praised for a "breakthrough" approach to political reform that liberalized and democratized the system at the risk of bringing down both communist rule and the Soviet Union itself, then Yeltsin can be praised for at least tackling the issue of economic reform in 1992—something Gorbachev never mustered the courage to do, and which was becoming a dire necessity by the end of 1991—though at the risk of impoverishing large numbers of citizens. If Gorbachev is praised for seeking a democratic federalism as the alternative to the Soviet unitary state, then Yeltsin can be praised for seeking an intermediate variant of center-regional relations ("asymmetrical federalism") as the alternative to both a unitary state and regional fragmentation. If Gorbachev is praised for resisting the temptation to "restore order" in the face of political challenges, then Yeltsin deserves some credit for retaining the civil liberties enacted under Gorbachev and for resisting the temptation to impose the kind of one-man dictatorship found in so many successor states of the former Soviet Union. None of this excuses Yeltsin's excesses. But it does put them in perspective.

And yet, having recorded all these caveats, it is certainly the case that Yeltsin's strategies for founding and guaranteeing a new order of things were insensitive to the costs of those strategies. Indeed, in his resignation speech of December 31, 1999, Yeltsin admitted as much.[25] Hence, we may argue that, if shock therapy was in any sense historically "necessary," the creation and indulgence of a corrupt, plutocratic elite, and the inattention to widespread immiseration, were not. If strong leadership was necessary, arbitrary leadership and the infantilizaton of political parties, judicial institutions, and parliament were not. If breaking the deadlock with the Supreme Soviet and adoption of a new constitution in 1993 were necessary, the promulgation of this particular constitution was not.[26] If defense of the territorial integrity of Russia was necessary, the wars in Chechnya were not. Indeed, the costs incurred by these policies may have contributed to the fragile condition in which Russia finds itself today—and are central to the indictment of Yeltsin as a leader who did not find a way to sustain his creation after his own inevitable departure.

Moreover, Yeltsin's strategy of political self-protection undercut whatever contribution he might have made to cultural transformation in Russia. He made an excellent start in 1990–1991 with his secular and tolerant rhetoric of Russian nationhood and statehood. But throughout 1989–1991, the absolutist rhetoric of anti-communism, based on binary oppositions, was the dominant and most salient feature of his rhetoric. The two rhetorics coexisted thereafter, and it was to Yeltsin's credit that he did not sacrifice the tolerant to the intolerant. But continuation of the absolutist rhetoric after the collapse of communism polluted political language and led to popular cynicism about the politics and policies of the Russian government. Thus, just as he had defined the Communist Party and the Soviet center variously as the enemy in 1989–1991, so he continued with "us versus them" rhetoric after 1991. Those who supported Yeltsin's policies were deemed "reformers," "democrats," and "marketizers," even when his policies were authoritarian, corrupt, or plutocratic. Those who opposed his policies were dubbed conservatives, reactionaries, or "neo-Bolsheviks."[27] These were not the rhetorical conditions under which the Russian citizenry was likely to learn to appreciate either markets or democracy—for the negative side effects of Yeltsin's policies, including the sustained failure to pay wage arrears and pensions, fostered cynicism about both capitalism and democracy in the minds of many Russians.

Yeltsin had the opportunity in 1991 to play the role of "father of the nation," embodying its dignity. Indeed, after the coup attempt of August 1991, this was both his self-image and his image in the eyes of anti-communist publics in Russia. But during his years as president of independent Russia, he managed to squander the good will he had accumulated. It is extraordinary to note the contrast between Yeltsin's popularity ratings and public demeanor in 1991 and the same indicators in 1994. In contrast to de Gaulle, who managed to mobilize French patriotism in support of his policies and leadership, Yeltsin could only neutralize or deter neo-imperial chauvinism. He proved incapable of articulating and broadcasting a positive, patriotic message to mobilize support for the kinds of popular sacrifices his policies demanded.

The net result of all these shortcomings is that the cultural and organizational infrastructures of the Russian system are extremely weak: like a skeleton without ligaments, they are prone to collapse of their own weight or when they meet countervailing force—such as the international economic downturn of August 1998. System-builders and the systems they build are frequently able to weather such times if they have created sufficient popular consensus and good will. But Yeltsin managed to squander his charisma and good will and later to discredit political and economic liberalism in the popular mind. Having discredited communism in his role as an oppositional revolutionary, and liberalism more recently, Yeltsin opened the door to the one ideology that had not yet been discredited: radical nationalism. Perhaps radical nationalism will not emerge ascendant, both because of the weak resonance of radical nationalism among the Russian people and the widespread awareness among elites of the country's real weakness. But if radical nationalism does seize the initiative, it could destroy Yeltsin's greatest ideational accomplishment—acceptance of a secular and tolerant definition of citizenship—along with the fragile organizational system he set up.

The Balance of the Ledger

Both Gorbachev and Yeltsin proved effective in advancing their negative goals: to undermine (Gorbachev) or destroy (Yeltsin) the old system. But both of them receive mixed grades for effectiveness in constructing the alternative systems that they envisaged. Whether these leaders are treated historically as tragic or myopic depends on the observer's estimation of whether they ever had a chance to succeed in these system-building endeavors. If, given the constraints, they could have done better, then they will be viewed as lacking the ability to achieve more. But if, given the constraints, they never stood a chance of succeeding, they could both be viewed as tragic and quixotic.

In the near term, they will both likely receive credit for heroic leadership in setting their countries on a new trajectory. In the long term, when we see whether Russia muddles through its crisis and avoids extremism or disorder, we may have a better view of whether each man's leadership, whatever its limitations, set the stage for a better or worse future. For, as Dean Acheson put it, "Sometimes it is only in retrospect and in the light of how things work out that you can distinguish stubbornness from determination."[28]

Notes

1. Stanley Hoffmann, "Heroic Leadership: The Case of Modern France," in *Political Leadership in Industrialized Societies,* ed. Lewis J. Edinger (New York: John Wiley & Sons, Inc., 1967), p. 113.

2. Jerry Hough, *The Logic of Economic Reform in Russia* (Washington, D.C.: Brookings Institution, 2001).

3. This is a rare person in Western scholarship; it is common among Russian journalists of a revanchist persuasion.

4. Prompting Chalmers Johnson to ask: "How many eggs do you have to break to make a one-egg omelette?" In "Foreword" of Alexander Dallin and George W. Breslauer, *Political Terror in Communist Systems* (Stanford, Calif.: Stanford University Press, 1970), p. vi.

5. Jerry Hough, *Revolution and Democratization in the USSR, 1985–1991* (Washington, D.C.: Brookings Institution, 1998).

6. See George W. Breslauer, "Evaluating Gorbachev as Leader," *Soviet Economy* 8, no. 4 (October-December 1989).

7. Peter Reddaway and Dmitri Glinsky, *The Tragedy of Russia's Reforms* (Washington, D.C.: U.S. Institute of Peace, 2001).

8. Anders Aslund, *How Russia Became a Market Economy* (Washington, D.C.: The Brookings Institution, 1995); Andrei Shleifer and Daniel Treisman, *Without a Map: Political Tactics and Economic Reform in Russia* (Cambridge, Mass.: The MIT Press, 2000).

9. This is a standard refrain by many scholars contributing to the Internet-based *Johnson's Russia List.*

10. This is a major theme of Leon Aron, *Yeltsin: A Revolutionary Life* (New York: St. Martin's, 2000); contrast this with Hough's depiction of the strength and orientations of the opposition, in *The Logic of Economic Reform.*

11. Historians tend to reject counterfactual analysis as a scholarly exercise, whereas social scientists often embrace it. Such historians include E. H. Carr, A. J. P. Taylor, and E. P. Thompson. For a book by social scientists that is devoted to the methodology and application of counterfactual reasoning in the study of international affairs, see Philip Tetlock and Aaron Belkin, eds., *Counterfactual Thought Experiments in World Politics* (Princeton: Princeton University Press, 1996).

12. See, for example, the special issue of *Time* magazine (13 April 1998) devoted to evaluation of 20th-century leaders.

13. See George Breslauer and Richard Ned Lebow, "Gorbachev, Reagan, and the End of the Cold War," unpublished manuscript, 2000.

14. The concept of "event-making man" is from Sidney Hook, *The Hero in History* (Boston: Beacon Press, 1943), p. 154.

15. Joseph Schumpeter, *Capitalism, Socialism, and Democracy* (New York and London: Harper & Brothers, 1942), pp. 81–86.

16. Observers who mourn Soviet loss of superpower status and control over Eastern Europe would not place the "end of the Cold War" in the "improvements" category.

17. For present purposes, I will treat the period March 1985 to late-August 1991 (i.e., through the coup attempt) as the "Gorbachev era." Thereafter, disintegrative trends accelerated sharply, and Gorbachev's political authority had all but evaporated.

18. A commission of inquiry, which included people closer to Yeltsin than to Gorbachev, exonerated Gorbachev from charges of having ordered the use of force (Archie Brown, *The Gorbachev Factor* [Oxford, UK: Oxford University Press, 1996], pp. 264–267); but it remains the case that he failed to prevent it.

19. Ronald Tiersky, "Perestroika and Beyond," *Problems of Communism* 39, no. 2 (1990): 114; *Time*, 4 June 1990, pp. 27–34.

20. Doig and Hargrove find this characteristic to be typical of successful leaders of the public bureaucracies they studied (Jameson W. Doig and Erwin C. Hargrove, eds., *Leadership and Innovation* [Baltimore, Md.: Johns Hopkins University Press, 1967], p. 19).

21. See Doder and Branson, *Gorbachev,* pp. 31, 304, and passim.

22. Ibid., pp. 31, 75, 106, 126–128, 157, 163, 218–219, 374–376, for examples. See also Brown, *The Gorbachev Factor,* chapters 4 and 7; and English, *Russia and the Idea of the West,* chapters 5 and 6. Henry Kissinger (*White House Years* [Boston: Little Brown, 1979], p. 54) has argued that "it is an illusion to believe that leaders gain in profundity while they gain experience. . . . The convictions that leaders have formed before reaching high office are the intellectual capital they will consume as long as they continue in office." The evolution of Gorbachev's thinking during his first five years in office challenges the applicability to his leadership of Kissinger's generalization. If that challenge is sustainable, it would strengthen a positive

evaluation of Gorbachev's leadership skills. Alternatively, one could argue that Gorbachev's "convictions" were fixed before he came to power and that his learning was largely "tactical" within the bounds of his earlier convictions. Part of the problem in deciding this is purely definitional. Does "conviction" refer to values alone or also to one's understandings about cause-effect relations within the domestic system, society, and international environment?

23. The concept comes from Hook, *The Hero in History.*

24. Yeltsin has been roundly condemned for his "shock therapy" approach to economic reform in 1992. But little attention has been given to the counterfactual: What would have been the consequences of an alternative strategy for dealing with the dire economic circumstances—both macroeconomic and microeconomic—at the time? Critics speak vaguely of "gradualism" or an "evolutionary" approach, without specification of how such a "policy" would have checked the economic crisis of late 1991. Strategies recommended by reformist Soviet economists for the stable conditions of 1986–1987 were not necessarily workable in the conditions of 1992. Hence, it is far from clear whether credible, alternative strategies were intellectually available and practicable when Yeltsin made his choice on behalf of shock therapy. Indeed, comparative analyses of postcommunist economic reform suggest that Yeltsin's mistake may have been the opposite: to back off from shock therapy after April 1992 in favor of a broader coalition among economic elites, thus miring Russia in a condition of partial reform that encourages massive corruption. See Joel Hellman, "Winners Take All: The Politics of Partial Reform in Postcommunist Transitions," *World Politics* 50, no. 2 (January 1998).

25. For the English-language text of this speech, see Boris Yeltsin, *Midnight Diaries* (New York: Public Affairs, 2000), pp. 386–387.

26. It is a separate question as to whether the tactics Yeltsin used to break the deadlock were necessary.

27. Hough, *The Logic of Economic Reform in Russia.* Yeltsin's rhetoric thus reinforced the mentality of "binary oppositions" that Michael Urban ("The Politics of Identity in Russia's Postcommunist Transition: The Nation Against Itself," *Slavic Review* 53, no. 3 [Fall 1994]: 733–766) claims to be a key feature of Russian political culture.

28. As quoted in Marshall D. Shulman, *The New York Review of Books,* 17 June 1990, p. 5.

4

From Yeltsin to Putin: The Evolution of Presidential Power

Lilia Shevtsova

Several preliminary conclusions about the extent to which Russia has succeeded in breaking away from past models of power and leadership and evolved along a liberal democratic path can be drawn from the past ten years of Russia's postcommunist experience and the transfer of presidential power that took place in March 2000. We are witness to a dramatic transformation that is filled with conflict, movements backward, attempts to reconcile what is uneasily reconciled, and the countless traps into which all political forces, without exception, have fallen.

The role of the leader in this transformation has been huge because of the way power has remained personified in Russia. Any leader in Russia, where change and reform are always carried out from the top down, would be faced with a dramatic choice: either preserve stability at the risk of bringing society to stagnation or degradation, or make a break with the past, never being certain whether the people will support such a break and not knowing how it will turn out.

The history of postcommunist leadership in Russia is the history of attempts to combine continuity and renewal—attempts not only to open up to the West and go beyond the bounds of autocratic power structures, but also to preserve the basic aspects of these structures, perhaps reflecting an unwillingness to fully abandon past patterns of authority. It is a history of hope, which ended in a financial crash yet at the same time demonstrated that both society and the leaders were able to overcome old patterns of political power. In this chapter, I attempt to analyze the basic characteristics of Yeltsin's leadership, the extent to which Vladimir Putin's leadership is a continuation of the Yeltsin past, and the degree to which Putin has broken with the ideology and type of rule of the Yeltsin era.

Yeltsin and His Political Project

Measuring Success and Failure

Boris Yeltsin's leadership can be judged from various perspectives. One can look at the results of his activities as a destroyer of the Soviet Union and communism, or one can examine how he managed to maintain stability in society. In both cases, he might receive high marks. If we next compare Russia's political situation in the communist period with that after its fall—with clear progress toward promoting freedoms, political pluralism, and regular elections—then Yeltsin could also be favorably judged. However, the evaluation of Yeltsin's leadership and legacy inevitably changes if the opportunities and chances that were wasted, including those for which he alone is to blame, are taken into account. If we thus evaluate the consequences of Yeltsin's actions from the point of view of how far he succeeded in moving Russia closer to liberal democracy and understood the need for proper legal structures and mechanisms to do so, then his leadership will be judged very harshly.

In this chapter we will examine Yeltsin's activities based on liberal-democratic criteria. Such an evaluation must take account of, first, his consistency in understanding the goals and principles of liberal democracy and, second, his plan of action for achieving these goals and principles. These two criteria, however, are not enough to adequately evaluate Yeltsin's leadership. For even a consistent liberal democrat in Russia can turn out to be a useless, ineffective ruler if he does not know how to build a democratic model in the national-historical context of society. Thus, it is necessary to include a third criterion to assess Yeltsin's leadership—namely, the degree to which he managed to regulate the relation between continuity and renewal and took into account Russian traditions and the readiness of both society and the political elite to accept a different model of development. On the basis of these criteria, we can draw conclusions about the costs of advancing society toward liberal democracy and of slowing down and failing along this path.

Indeed, a revolutionary advance toward liberal democracy at any price, without considering the mood of society—what might be termed "liberal Bolshevism"—could only discredit reform. But, on the other hand, there was opportunity for a deeper democratic breakthrough in Russia, and it was missed because of the leader's inability to gauge society's readiness to break from traditional models of government, his excessive compromises with the old part of the elite, and his refusal to renew the elite in the end.

As far as Yeltsin's understanding of the principles of liberal democracy is concerned, everything points to his clearly recognizing the need for market reform as the sole factor that could lead Russia from the deep economic crisis that accompanied the collapse of communism. During the fight for power with Soviet central authorities, headed by Mikhail Gorbachev, Yeltsin gave the impression of being a person who understood the need for giving the authorities democratic legitimacy and securing political freedoms, in particular, freedom of the press. Moreover, in the process of his rise to the top, Yeltsin demonstrated that he knew how to make use of these freedoms. But when he came to power, Yeltsin changed his mind about what Russia needed. "Everything should be subordinate to a single, sharply defined principle, law, establishment. Roughly speaking, someone in the country should be chief. That's all there is to it," he wrote.[1] Another telling declaration was: "I act the way I consider necessary."[2] Well, what kind of democracy is that?

If democratic behavior means a leader's ability to engage in dialogue with opponents and willingness to make compromises, then it would be hard to find a politician less disposed than Yeltsin to making any kind of concessions to reach agreement. Russia does not need compromises, he said, but a "stronger, stricter, even more coercive politics."[3] Yeltsin viewed all kinds of mutual concessions not as a sign of good sense but of weakness, cowardice, and decline. His aversion to compromise did not mean that Yeltsin generally did not make concessions; but it was done solely as an element of his strategy for personal survival.

Yeltsin apparently was prepared to tolerate democracy as long as it did not threaten his position, and he was ready to either renounce or ignore the most important principles of democracy (although not without wavering) in defense of his own power.[4] Consequently, his relationship to democracy rather depended on the situation and correlation of forces.

That Yeltsin disregarded obligations to the democratic forces in Russia that supported his rise to power also played a certain role. These forces were so weak and uncoordinated that they could not exert pressure on Yeltsin when he began to shape the contours of the new regime.[5]

As for a clear plan for reform, Yeltsin and those close to him never had one. Yeltsin was an intuitive and spontaneous politician who did not always think about the consequences of his first step, rarely thought about the next one, and did not think in the long term at all.[6] An indication of Yeltsin's attitude toward the process of building a new government is his relationship to the work of the constitutional commission in 1991, of which he was, by the way, the leader: not once did Yeltsin attend a meeting. His behavior amounted to a lack of understanding of the role that the constitution played in the changes that Russia had effected. However, the way he immediately acted after the collapse of Soviet institutions in fall 1991 leads to the conclusion that he preferred to consolidate his power through coercion and pressure rather than through political reform and long-term agreements with other forces. During the first stage of the transformation, when the fate of the new political reality of Russia was being decided, he showed no interest in building new institutions or working out a strategy for development. Yeltsin began to implement economic reforms before the institutions of political power were established, not only because of the perilous state of the economy but also because of his scorn for planned and systemic work in carrying out reform. He had hoped as well that power could be consolidated by autocratic means. Democratic games, Yeltsin and those near him thought, could only lead to a loss of power.

Several statements by Yeltsin reveal his style of leadership. "Making a decision, I throw myself as if into water," he wrote. "I don't want to analyze whether this is a shortcoming or asset."[7] While governing such a huge country, especially one in a period of transformation rather than stabilization, this quality is clearly a shortcoming. He also wrote: "Play only to win."[8] Such decisiveness is praiseworthy. But with Yeltsin, decisiveness often turned into stubbornness and disregard for the cost of victory.

Yeltsin had astonishing political intuition, allowing him at decisive moments to grasp the mood of the people and make the right decisions, at least as far as the logic of power was concerned. But he was absolutely incapable of carrying out the routine work of defining tactics or setting goals and attaining them. Having fought for power, Yeltsin returned to governing the country only when a serious crisis arose. The rest of the time he was busy following behind-the-scenes intrigues of his court and neutralizing possible opponents. Everything he did was done by fits and starts, depending on the circumstances and interests involved in the running battles. He was a reactive and impulsive politician.[9]

Let us now turn to the question of how Yeltsin combined continuity and change. Yeltsin's very political nature in the way he behaved embodied both the characteristics of a typical Soviet politician and the desire to destroy the communist past within himself.

On the one hand, he could act like a *barin*, a lord, and treat his subordinates with arrogance. He preferred to make decisions behind the scenes and on his own. He would not tolerate criticism and opposition. He could not function in a situation in which there was a division of power, and he strove to monopolize power completely. He treated power as his own property and could not stand others' making claims to it.

But, on the other hand, Yeltsin could show a democratic side. He understood the meaning of freedoms and did not encroach on them. He knew how to address society directly in his fight against the bureaucracy and his opponents, and he understood the power of society.

As a result, not only the style but also the politics of this first Russian president were contradictory. Yeltsin made anticommunism his ideology and he was able to accustom the political elite to operate in an atmosphere of pluralism. Further, he gave his first government to young and unknown liberal technocrats, which was a break with the Russian tradition of gerontocracy. At the same time, nevertheless, his leadership was formed on a tsarist basis.

Bridging Incompatibilities

In essence, Yeltsin managed to become a transformational leader thanks to his mixed political nature. He turned out to be a rebel who emerged from the depths of the old system while still belonging to it. It is difficult to imagine the dissident Andrey Sakharov as the leader of the new Russia. Someone like Vaclav Havel or Lech Walesa is absolutely unthinkable for Russia. Their coming to power in Czechoslovakia and Poland reflected a rather wide experience with a certain decompression of the former regime, which was accomplished while the countries were still under communism.

Russia, however, had to carry out liberalization and democratization at the same time, and therefore in many ways the country needed a leader who could unite two parts of society: those who were not yet ready to part entirely with Soviet life and thus wanted partial reform and those who wanted to break with the past as quickly as possible. True, another path toward overcoming communism was theoretically possible: a reliance on the revolutionary, anticommunist section of society and a radical uprooting of all Soviet elements, including a change in the elite and the construction of new institutions. But such a radical transformation would demand above all a leadership prepared to neutralize the parts of society not ready for decisive changes. This kind of transformation would have required at the very least large, organized liberal forces that had a plan of action. Besides, even if a radical transformation from the top were successfully carried out on the surface, one could expect that within a short time the cultural milieu, historical particularities, traditions, and political stereotypes and habits would begin to impair the new institutions. By discussing the contradictory essence of Yeltsin's leadership and the limitations that he apparently could not overcome, I am in no way trying to justify Yeltsin as a leader and the path that he chose. It is a question of trying to understand the nature of these limitations while avoiding emotional criticism.

A peaceful approach to transforming Russia apparently required a form of leadership that would attempt to unite conflicting, often incompatible aspirations and become a rallying point during the transition from the old model of development. For an evolutionary transition from communism, while the country still lacked a consensus regarding the past, present, and future, Russia needed a leader of a special sort, a politician of great charisma, who could, albeit temporarily, consolidate society in order to implement its first reforms. Such a leader could embody both the legacy of the past, which would make him acceptable to the conservative part of society, and the desire to put an end to that legacy, which would give hope to the reformist part of the population. Such a leader-consolidator would have to personify both transition and a desire to move ahead. He could not be ideologically rigid or even clearly defined: he was bound to vacillate, have weaknesses, and explode over conflicts. Such a contradictory, inconsistent leadership, perhaps, would be a guarantee for a relatively peaceful exit from communism. But the cost of this course of events inevitably would be to slow down liberal-democratic change. Of course, the optimal course for Russia would be if Yeltsin had been the leader during the stage at which communism was overcome, and then he had been followed by a more decisive leader who was capable of understanding the aims of liberal democracy and of uniting the nation on a democratic platform. But, alas, it happened otherwise, and Yeltsin stayed on the political scene too long, when the need for an anti-communist consolidator had faded and he had already turned into an obstacle to a new stage of reform.

It should be noted that the contradictoriness of the political nature and experience of Yeltsin was only one of the factors that defined the essence of his leadership. Historical circumstances also influenced his rule, some of which strengthened his democratic proclivities, while others made him resort to stereotypical authoritarian-monarchist behavior. Some of the circumstances that initially facilitated Yeltsin's democratic tone of leadership include the continued democratic upsurge in society during 1991; the weakening and discrediting of communist and nationalist forces; the desire of a significant portion of the people to draw closer to the West; and society's readiness to make sacrifices in the name of reform.

Let's now turn to the obstacles that slowed the development of democratic aspects of Yeltsin's term in office. Among them is the need for conducting political and economic reforms and at the same time building a new state. The lack of consensus on the basic parameters of the new state held back both the formation of a market and democratization. Democratic process requires the existence of many state institutions, but there is not enough evidence yet—from the Czech and Slovak republics, for example—to argue that combining democratization with state-building might be successful. Furthermore, reforms in Russia were carried out in a cultural milieu that in many ways rejected them.[10]

But the most serious obstacle complicating Yeltsin's democratic leadership was the lack in Russia of influential forces that would try to dismember monolithic power and find a way out of the old autocracy. Even those who called themselves liberal and democratic while the new Russia was still being formed thought along the lines of a one-power system and dreamed of an authoritarian "presidential vertical" chain of authority. They made no attempts to convince Yeltsin of the need to create independent institutions. In fact, the new ruling class linked strengthening its authority and even market reform with the establishment of an "iron hand" in the country.

The desire to preserve Russia's status as a superpower also played a great role in society (especially among the political elites). This desire encouraged the preservation of old messianic, state-power, and imperialist illusions, making the transition to a new way of political thinking and new forms of leadership more difficult.

What is noteworthy is the remarkable inability of certain elite groups in the new Russia to reach agreement on the basic questions of future development. Pacts and compromises along the lines of the ones made in Spain, Poland, Hungary, and even South Africa turned out to be impossible in Russia. The fact that "polarized pluralism" (to use the expression of Giovanni Sartori) has also been characteristic of other countries—in particular, of the French elite after the Fifth Republic, which for almost a quarter-century learned the art of compromise—is of no comfort. The precedent of the fall of the Weimar Republic, which was in many ways the result of an inability on the part of elite groups to reach agreement, thus opening the way for extremist forces, is an all-too-memorable warning. In Russia the dissension within and fragmentation of the political elite turned out to be an ideal ground for the establishment of personality-based leadership, which became a compensation for an unconsolidated elite.

The question should be asked: Could Yeltsin under such a combination of favorable circumstances and obstacles have moved further in the direction of liberal democracy than he did? Theoretically, yes. But that Yeltsin did not know how and thus did not manage (did not want?) to do so was a consequence not only of resistance from external factors, but also the influence of his own experience and his understanding of the essence of power and of the goals that he set for himself. True, he shares responsibility for the slowing of democratic reforms with the democrats and liberals who preferred to build democracy in Russia by supporting a new monarch.

To what degree was Yeltsin a revolutionary, a reformer, and a destroyer of the old system? Was he a democrat, liberal, authoritarian statist, Westernizer, nationalist? Yeltsin's moves, numerous transformations, and changes of political clothing showed his ability to fill almost any role during his two terms in office. He destroyed and tried to create. He embodied through his politics and the very fact of being in power a link to the past, while at the same time he was a destroyer, having put an end to the Soviet state. Depending on the circumstances and firmness of his positions, Yeltsin was ready to take liberal steps or to cross over to a *dirigiste* style of rule. He could give speeches like a Westernizer, and then make extreme statements about great-state power.

Yeltsin changed before everyone's eyes, following a path that would have been utterly unthinkable for him five to ten years earlier. He turned out to be a very dynamic politician who was able to make rather significant progress by virtue of the fact, above all, that he did not have clear convictions and ideological taboos. His ideology was the fight for power.

At the same time, it would be a simplification to reduce the entire Yeltsin leadership only to his movement to the top, to his desire for power. At the very least, at the initial stage of his leadership in 1990–1991, one could sense in his behavior a desire to leave the past behind and turn the face of Russia toward the West, toward Europe. But starting in 1992, his behavior as a leader was in many ways determined by the logic of fighting for and acquiring power. If liberal-democratic principles made self-preservation easier, then he followed them. If those principles posed a threat to his power, he either ignored or repudiated them. The most convincing example of his relationship to liberal democracy was his relations with the parliament. From the very start, Yeltsin viewed the institution itself as a threat to his role and a limitation on his rights to power. This, above all, and not differences in ideological positions, determined his sharply negative relations with the legislative authorities.

Governing by Instinct

After he came to power, following the failure of the coup attempt in August 1991, Yeltsin's original goal was the creation of the "presidential vertical" chain of authority—meaning his own authoritarian or semi-authoritarian regime, which was to be based on a market economy and which would work by relying on cadres loyal to him. What arose as a result of his rule looks on the surface like a superpresidential republic, but the pyramid structure of the regime conceals its complex contents. In essence, what arose was a hybrid regime in which the most contradictory of components were combined—democracy, authoritarianism, oligarchy, and the elements of autocracy that were traditional in pre-Soviet Russia.

The establishment of the Yeltsin regime was preceded by a torturous period of dual power between 1991 and 1993, which was characterized by confrontation between the executive and legislative powers. Given the lack of a real multiparty system at this time, both branches of power turned out to form a kind of mega-party system, reflecting conflicting aspirations—liberal and technocratic versus populist and nationalist—that tore Russian society apart during this time. But the basis of the opposition between the branches was a struggle for the preservation of Russia's traditional model of power, which made reconciliation doubtful.

The dissolution of the parliament in 1993 gave the president and his team the opportunity to begin implementing his plan for creating an "elected monarchy." The new Yeltsin constitution became not an agreement between society and the authorities, but a manifesto of the victorious side. The people were forced to approve this manifesto in a referendum that presented no alternatives other than existing without a constitution at all. The way in which the constitution of 1993 was prepared (Yeltsin himself was in charge of drafting it and also made amendments to it) and adopted, by exerting pressure on the opposition, resulted in a fundamental law based not on the initiative of the people, where power rests, but on the initiative of those in power, and above all the leader, who "gave birth" to the constitution.[11] As a matter of fact, the same process had occurred during previous stages of Russian and Soviet development—in 1906, 1936, and 1976, when the tsarist, Stalin, and Brezhnev constitutions were adopted. Thus, the Yeltsin presidential regime arose not from the will of the people or a revolution, but in the course of an anti-parliamentary overthrow led by Yeltsin, which could not but have influenced its further development.

While the new Russian regime was being formed, previous sources of legitimacy—armed force, the party, ideology, and monarchic succession—appeared to be exhausted. Under those conditions, it was the democratic legitimization of power through elections that became the most important means for preserving and generating this power. At the same time the democratically elected authorities began to function like a quasi-monarchy. The combination of political succession and its repudiation made up the essence of the Yeltsin regime and simultaneously the regime's basic internal contradictions.

While the new political structures were being put in place, an old quality of Russian political mentality emerged. The well-known Russian monarchist Lev Tikhomirov, who established the theory of Russian monarchy, had already noticed this quality. He wrote that the Russian people, including its educated representatives, had developed strong political instincts because of the almost complete absence of political consciousness.[12]

The predominance of instinct over political consciousness is reflected in the attention paid by those in Russia who govern to the individuals who occupy government posts rather than to the painstaking work of organizing political authority and forming the principles of that authority. From this orientation stems the famous distinctiveness of Russia's understanding of power: its strengths and drawbacks are associated not as much with its organization as with the personal strengths and drawbacks of the people who occupy certain positions.

Because the founding fathers of the United States understood that it is better not to rely on human virtues but to be guided by the less exalted idea of the selfishness of human nature, they constructed a system of institutions under which the selfishness of each person would curb the selfishness of others. The French model of government, which was founded on faith in human virtue, proceeds from the conscious aspiration to make the people, and not the ruling class, the source of power, as the consequence of conclusions drawn from the experience of tyranny.[13] Russian political culture, even after the fall of communism and the recognition of the sad experience of totalitarianism, turned out to be absolutely unsuited to building a structure of authority or deriving authority from the people. To this day, Russians have yet to be able to think about how powers should be divided among institutions, how to balance them, and how they could be controlled by the people.

Therefore, it is very strange to hear discussions on the part of some Russian intellectuals about how almost all the ills of postcommunist Russia stem from the fact that the country borrowed from Western political institutions while ignoring the particularities of Russian political culture.[14] In fact, Western norms and institutions have constantly been adapted and subordinated to Russian culture, and building on them has always been secondary. Thus, only those elements of the American and French models of power that guaranteed the authority of the highest post in government were adopted during the building of Yeltsin's regime, and everything that could limit his power was rejected. When the new regime was being formed, the main question was the same as before: To whom does all power belong? After Yeltsin, the main question remains: Who should rule Russia and who should become its savior? Russian political (and economic) history of the past decade has still been created instinctively rather than consciously. Therefore, instead of a democratic political system in Russia, a pyramid regime has arisen, at the head of which, as before, is a leader with authoritarian aspirations trying to guarantee reproduction of his power. Cool heads would have been needed from the start for a viable new system to take shape. But for Russian heads, even the most enlightened ones, this was not the case.[15] Yeltsin is one of the clearest examples of a politician who ruled by instinct, which was particularly developed when it came to holding on to power. Instinct also rules those who count themselves as democrats and liberals but continue to put their trust in the leader, in turn reducing themselves to the role of members of a monarch's court or of a marginalized section if the autocrat excludes them from the circle of insiders.

It should be noted, however, that the attempt to preserve personal rule with strong patrimonial features in a new situation and a pluralistic society is a complex problem, for it entails preserving this rule in the presence of a democratic system of legitimizing power—which is to say elections. In this situation the leaders have intuitively, without reflection, found what seemed to them a tried and true solution: they attempted to maximize the powers of the leader (concentrating them in the presidency) and to minimize responsibility for that power. But sharing responsibility without sharing real powers is very complicated. Such a deal turned out to be possible in Russia only under one condition: if the division of responsibility became a sharing of irresponsibility. This led to the development of a regime in Russia, at the head of which was an all-powerful leader, who thought only of how to control all the levers of power, but who was not responsible for anything. The same occurred on all other levels of authority—at the level of the subjects of the federation and at the local and city levels, where local barons came to power but refused to accept responsibility for their actions. Both civil society and the judicial system were too weak to make them accountable.

How should the Yeltsin regime be compared with other transitional regimes that have also included hybrid elements?[16] The regime can be likened to a constitutionally "elected monarchy" that comprehends its conditional character. Defining the Russian regime in this way puts it in a national-historical context and shows the presence of tradition and, at the same time, a sharp rupture with it.[17] It allows us to determine what is central to Russian authority: the preservation of the power of the leadership and the need to make it democratically legitimate.

The regime created by Yeltsin was in many ways a reflection of his contradictory nature, in which a constantly democratic-populist beginning came into conflict with an authoritarian-monarchistic one.[18] In this connection it can be said that the new power in Russia is now even more personalized than it was under communism. On one hand, the conflict between democratic and authoritarian beginnings created the opportunity, or the illusion, that it could develop in the most diverse directions—authoritarian as well as democratic. On the other hand, this conflict turned into a source of internal instability for the authorities and prevented them from rallying around a single system of values. Moreover, the combination of democracy and personalistic rule with elements of tsarist tradition could not help but lead to the discrediting of democracy and conversion of it into a façade that hid an entirely different substance inside.

At the core of the Yeltsin regime was a leader who put himself above the political scene and concentrated all the main levers of power in his hands, while serving as a guarantor of the stability of society. The personalized model of leadership has existed in Russia over the course of many centuries, varying only in its ideological orientation and sources of legitimacy. Under the communist state, the personalized rule received its legitimacy from the party and hid behind a mask of collective leadership, which changed its essence very little. Under Yeltsin, a tradition was restored that had long distinguished Russia from the rest of Europe: power vested in a single subject became the principal nucleus of politics, destroying all independent subjects, which from then on could be free to act only on instructions from this single subject.[19] After Yeltsin left power, there was an increased tendency of all actors on the Russian political scene to begin reproducing this subjective authority in a presidency that takes the place of the previous party-state.

Within the logic of the "elected monarchy," the leader is the main subject, who has his own logic, engenders his own authority, and delegates some powers to other subjects. It is this power, and not the people, that is the main focus of the constitution. Power that is based on a repetition of Russian tradition does not allow for the possibility of placing Russia fully within the context of Western civilization.[20] Furthermore, the subjective character of Russian authority and its personification facilitated the carrying out of market reforms, which required neutralizing opposition from various social groups that were not ready to give up state paternalism. But at the same time, the return of subjective power made creating systemic politics in Russia, that is, a whole complex of independent institutions, impossible. Therefore, by focusing all power exclusively on the area of market reform, Russia in the final analysis lost the strategic battle of creating a liberal democratic society. Moreover, the market infrastructure began to become deformed as a result of the lack of necessary systemic components of liberal democracy (for example, the rule of law).

But personalized leadership was not the only defining characteristic of the Yeltsin regime. At a certain level, the personalized type of leadership was a response to blocs from the past that remain part of the Russian political scene. These landowning-patrimonial, ideocratic, military-police, and bureaucratic blocs have made up the fabric of Russian political life over centuries.[21] The blocs were distinguished by their origins: some were born of the Slavonic tradition, others were the consequence of Tatar, Byzantine, and Prussian traditions. These blocs came into conflict with one another, but in a surprising way they lived through and survived postcommunism. True, in the course of postcommunist development, the ideological bloc managed to be neutralized, although possibly only temporarily.[22] The very existence of conflicting blocs required a leader and arbiter who could regulate relations among them and guarantee stability in society. To be fair, it should be pointed out that the arbiter in Russia often acted as the most progressive force, which restrained somewhat the conservatism of certain blocs, especially regarding their repressive security and regional forces.

Of course, the postcommunist leadership lacked certain autocratic attributes that formerly existed, and was mitigated by the electoral procedures that formed it. Therefore, any direct parallels between postcommunist Russia and feudal Russia are very relative. Moreover, the combination of traditional blocs of political reality with new realities could give rise to new challenges that old Russia has not known. The former sources of legitimizing authority—the party and security forces that were founded on the legacy of monarchism—could no longer help resolve the problem in Yeltsin's Russia of reproducing the ruling class. Democratically held elections created a situation of uncertainty for the authorities, which they had always wanted to avoid. In short, under conditions of postcommunism, the goals of the Russian ruling class were the same as in the past, but it was no longer possible to use previous methods to reach them.

Paradoxes of the Yeltsin Leadership

One of the most important qualities of the Yeltsin regime was its nonsystemic nature.[23] Of course in Russia there are certain elements of a political system, but a system as an aggregate of more or less independent institutions acting on the basis of clear rules of the game has not yet come into being. Russian power relies above all on one aspect of politics: a presidency under which other institutions are amorphous and insignificant and the division of functions among them is weak. Furthermore, the main requirement for the functioning of power is a contradictory system of values that includes mutually exclusive principles. All this, taken together, casts doubt on the systemic nature of Russian authority.

The nonsystemic character of the regime is proof that even after the fall of communism such an element of the past as the Communist Party, which up to one-third of the electorate supported at the elections, remains a major political force in Russia. In addition, the Communist Party plays a dual and very contradictory role. On the one hand, it is an element of the past and thus is an anti-regime force. But on the other, its very existence (at least during the time of Yeltsin) helped the regime function because it used anti-communist rhetoric in order to survive. The real or imaginary threat of a strong Communist Party is still the main obstacle to forming a strong democratic opposition to the regime.

Can there be a stable regime when it includes anti-regime elements that are not based on a consensus over basic principles of its existence? Paradoxically, the nonsystemic nature of the regime and shifts in models of power allowed it to advance and put down resistance to it, for it is impossible to resist what is not formed. But in the future, this nonsystemic character, lack of clear orientation, amorphous institution of leadership, and presence of mutually exclusive elements in its structure will become destabilizing factors.

Gradually it became evident that Russian authority could hardly help consolidate the powers and resources in a few hands. In fact, it turned out that the very process of consolidating these resources was an illusion, for the president was forced constantly to pay for the loyalty of some forces, the neutrality of others, and the suppression of yet others through the distribution of power. The main principle of the workings of power of Yeltsin was that of mutual connivance and mutual tolerance. Yeltsin apparently recognized that he did not have the necessary instruments for a vertical regulation of his power and therefore began to follow the slogan "Live and let live." The constant barters and deals for distributing power and property became the principal means of survival of the Yeltsin regime in general and the president in particular.

The agreements reached between the central authorities and the regions, in which the regions were often indulged and thus allowed to go beyond the bounds of the constitution, were the first example of how the leader traded power for the sake of self-preservation. These deals started a process of devolution of power from the center to the regions, which, however, had little in common with democratization. In the regions began to be formed semi-feudal regimes run by local princelings whose charter of immunity was their loyalty to the higher official in the government.

The principle of mutual connivance further extended to the relationship between the central authorities and influential economic groups. The loans-for-shares schemes, in the course of which court oligarchs received tasty morsels of state property as a reward for their support of Yeltsin during the 1996 elections, were the most obvious example of how deals worked. Such deals allowed the authorities to survive and offered influential groups maximum freedom to pursue their selfish interests.

As a result, the president's subjective authority became diluted. Having drained his sources of power, the president was incapable of carrying out decisions without making new deals with separate interest groups in the center and the regions. The result was a devaluation of the role and influence of the institution of the presidency. The outwardly powerful presidency turned out, in fact, to be impotent omnipotence. The continued support of the single-subject rule of the Yeltsin leadership could be achieved in two ways—either by further devaluation of power and weakening of the center (but then the subjective quality of this authority itself would disappear and power would flow to new centers) or by a forceful and administrative return of power to the center. Yeltsin did not decide on the latter.

Moreover, it soon became obvious that consolidating this power was simply impossible, for only the fragility and fragmentation of both the authorities and society would allow for a leader who could settle conflicts. Thus, Yeltsin was forced—owing to certain character traits but above all to the logic of his own regime—constantly to produce tension and encourage disturbances to give himself the opportunity to play the role of conciliator.

Yet another element of Yeltsin's means of survival was the system of shadowy checks and balances, which compensated for the lack of effective institutions and at the same time gave him the opportunity to remain on the surface of various group interests. At various stages of Yeltsin's presidency, he introduced into his system the group of Moscow Mayor Yury Luzhkov, the industrial group of Viktor Chernomyrdin, the liberal technocrats headed by Anatoly Chubais and Boris Nemtsov, and the security forces headed by Alexander Korzhakov and Mikhail Barsukov. Under such a system of informal lobbying, the marginal aspirations of certain interest groups could and at times did gain the upper hand. The system of informal checks, based on the proximity of certain groups of influence to the throne, was the consequence of paternalism and favoritism, and at the same time provoked their rise. At first, Yeltsin managed to keep his inner circle under control. But because of the president's weakening physical condition and his isolation, the "tail began to wag the dog," and the president became more and more clearly hostage to his monarchical court.

The Yeltsin regime thrived in an atmosphere of artificially prolonged revolutionary cycles. Not knowing how to consolidate power on the basis of consensus, Yeltsin prolonged indefinitely the period of shake-ups, constantly changing the government and his inner circle. He thus resolved the problem of responsibility: putting the blame on the mistakes and blunders of departing comrades-in-arms and creating the image of an enemy also made it easier for him to escape accountability. It is this avoidance of responsibility that explains his reshuffling of prime ministers. During his eight years in office, Yeltsin named seven prime ministers: Yegor Gaidar, Chernomyrdin (twice), Sergey Kirienko, Yevgeny Primakov, Sergey Stepashin, and Vladimir Putin.[24] True, at the same time, while playing prime-minister poker, Yeltsin solved yet another problem: the search for a successor. The prime minister in the Russian hierarchy is the first claimant to the post of president.

An essential element of the Yeltsin regime was the demonstrative lack of ideology, anticommunism being its only ideological aspect. But in everything else Yeltsin could move in various directions and combine various ideologies—Westernization, liberal democracy, open authoritarianism, statism, and elements of nationalism. It is only natural that a regime that is a hybrid would rely not only on an eclectic ideology but also on a diverse political and social base. Thus, the regime was supported by groups with varied and at times opposing aspirations—liberals, democrats, statists, pragmatists, great-power advocates, and at certain moments even nationalists. Yeltsin and his team could turn their attention at various points to different groups of influence, incorporate them into their circle, borrow their slogans, and then throw them out of the circle when they were no longer needed. The ideological omnivorousness, politics of constant compromises, and support from diverse groups added up to a way of preventing the rise of an influential opposition. Of course, without compromises and drawing various groups into power, especially pragmatists and representatives of the raw-materials industry, it would have been impossible to guarantee firm authority. But the fact still remains that the "spider's web" of checks was created by Yeltsin above all for the exclusive purpose of increasing his power rather than advancing reform.

The significant role that the young liberal technocrats played in shoring up Yeltsin's leadership should be particularly noted. The inclusion of

Chubais, Boris Fedorov, Gaidar, Nemtsov, and others in the structure of the single-subject regime gave it a modern look, helped it make certain if not always decisive or consistent steps toward reform, and sorted out minor conflicts. It should also be pointed out, however, that their coming to power obstructed the formation of a real democratic opposition and in the end discredited democratic and liberal values. Still, without them, Russia would not have taken the cautious steps toward market reforms that it has. But as for the prospects for liberal democracy in Russia, the strategic decision to bring the liberal technocrats to power brought more harm than good.

The fragmentation of society and the political elite, which artificially supported the center, was a large resource for the regime Yeltsin created. Yet another source of survival of power was the many conflicts at all stages and on all levels. These essentially reduced the threat of a bipolar confrontation from within the regime or between the regime and the people.

One of the results of the Yeltsin leadership was the formation around him of a special interest group, which on the one hand received benefits from its proximity to power and, on the other, helped certain powerful representatives find ways of personally enriching themselves. We are talking here of the oligarchs, although it should be noted that how they are defined is very relative. Oligarchs in Russia appeared the moment the presidency began to weaken. Having granted the authorities their financial and intellectual resources during the 1996 presidential elections, they were able to become elements of Yeltsin's base of support. Later the oligarchs tried to consolidate their hold within the regime as a systemic element and gain control over not only a portion of the country's economic resources, but the political process as well. The oligarchs partly succeeded in doing so, albeit for a short period.[25]

Subsequent events—even under Putin—showed that the oligarchic character of the regime created by Yeltsin could be temporary and provisional. Although the Russian regime grew dependent on certain groups, it could, in the final analysis, rid itself of this burden of dependence. As soon as one group or another began to demonstrate too much ambition or pretensions to an independent role, the leader could instantly produce an "anti-oligarchic revolution." This did not mean a return of the regime to democratic grounds. It only meant that in the framework of the presidential "vertical" power structure the leader could free himself from dependence on his group of supporters.

After another group of oligarchs was cast aside, the president could again attract new interest groups and give them the opportunity to become oligarchs in turn. But they, too, would be doomed if they began to make claims to an independent political role. In any case, we should not exaggerate the prospects of the Russian oligarchy and the possibility of their turning into a supporting element of the regime. The oligarchy will be doomed every time to serve, above all, the single-subject authority and, second, the bureaucracy. It is the bureaucracy that is the most important systemic element of the regime, without which it truly could not survive.[26] It is this dependence of the oligarchy on the state apparatus and its parasitical reliance on state resources that differentiates the Russian oligarchy as a social phenomenon from the oligarchs that make up an important component of the bureaucratic-authoritarian regimes in Latin America.

Yeltsin's rule also showed that, when the role of the leader is diminished, there is an inevitable strengthening of the role of the court—the president's close circle, others around him, and certain persons who play a compensatory role when the leader is weakened. When the leader suffers senile infirmity, favorites can play an important role as did, for example, the bodyguard Alexander Korzhakov in Yeltsin's court. If the "elected monarchy" is altogether shaky, then favoritism can turn into Rasputinism. Lacking institutional support, absolute rule always gravitates, under any leader, toward favoritism.[27] But those who aspired to become favorites had to know that they received their role only because it was temporary. Only a constant change in favorites could guarantee authority vested in one person and preserve his power from being usurped by the next favorite or group of oligarchs.

Thus, on the one hand, Yeltsin's leadership gravitated away from functional relations and toward personal ones based on complete trust. But on the other hand, the president inevitably came up against the fact that no one could be trusted. Needing devotion, at the same time he constantly expected betrayal. It was then that he turned to nepotism, drawing his family members into the circle of power, for only they, in their understanding of the leader, would not betray him, but would remain loyal. Therefore, it was the family that became the main bulwark and safety net for the leader, especially if he became inadequate, sick, or weak. Yeltsin's daughter, Tatyana Dyachenko, for example, was included in the circle of power, which strengthened the semi-monarchical character of the regime itself and at the same time became an indication of its degradation. "I am very grateful to Tanya that she never played in politics. She simply helped her father," Yeltsin said lovingly about his daughter.[28] Tatyana Dyachenko truly did not *play* in politics: she actively engaged in them. It was she who, during the last stage of Yeltsin's presidency, essentially played the role of an informal vice president.

In principle, nepotism is often an inevitable stage in the development of patriarchal regimes similar to Yeltsin's. The aspiration of the leader's family to influence the choice of a successor is always a consequence of nepotism, and thus provides a guarantee of his safety in the future. In short, nepotism increases the challenges to the remaining institutions of democracy.

The Decline of the Presidency

Yeltsin's governing provoked the formation of a stagnating rhythm of development, which was an ideal means of his survival. This form of government, nevertheless, could not successfully cope with crisis situations. Thus, after Yeltsin survived the August crash of 1998 with difficulty, he was forced to allow a change in his rule for the sake of avoiding either a collapse or the coming to power of a harsh dictatorship.[29] For Russia, this was an unprecedented experiment, of which researchers have still not taken sufficient account. What was involved is that in order for Yeltsin to get out of a political dead end, he agreed, albeit under duress, to transfer some power to the new prime minister, Yevgeny Primakov. The prime minister and government in turn began to rely on the parliament. For the first time in the country's postcommunist history, the prime minister became the main center of power. After the long period of one-person rule in Russia (with the exception of the period between 1991 and 1993), a system of dual power arose within the executive branch. This dual power, which rested on the responsibility of the prime minister for the current political and economic course with the president playing a safeguarding role, helped the country overcome the economic crisis and maintain stability. True, Russia's political elite did not thus succeed in increasing this division of power through legislative means. But most important, this dual leadership did not allow the ruling higher-ups to guarantee that their power would be reproduced. It was above all for this reason that Primakov was dismissed and the situation returned to its earlier state.[30]

Many analysts have viewed this period, during which one of the leaders of the Communist Party (Yury Maslyukov) was included in the government and the government itself relied on the leftist majority in the State Duma, as a retreat to the past and even a communist restoration. In fact, this situation involved something else: For the first time in Russia there was a divi-

sion of power, however partial, which was a departure from the limits of traditional autocracy. The experience of this on its own was of unquestionably
positive significance.

True, many would dispute such an interpretation, saying that the division
of power in Russia would lead to the appearance of conflicts between the
two centers of influence, to a "tug-of-war" between the president and prime
minister that inevitably would take place. It seems to me, however, that the
preservation of the traditional monolith of undivided power and the constant threat of authoritarianism are far more dangerous. The appearance of
an independent government with its own legitimacy that relies on the parliament could at first lead to a more cautious economic course. But in the
future, the very fact that both the parliament and the government would
share responsibility for the consequences of their policies would promote
optimal solutions to problems. The mere fact that Primakov's government,
including the communists, adopted for the first time in Russia a liberal budget, ratified by the leftist Duma, which had unexpectedly renounced populism, attests to the likelihood of such a course of events.

How and when the change of leaders occurred is of the utmost importance in understanding the essence of Yeltsin's rule. Yeltsin stepped down
from office early and voluntarily on December 31, 1999. In his televised
broadcast to Russia, Yeltsin said: "I made a decision. I thought about it long
and hard. Today, on the last day of the passing century, I submit my resignation." Wiping away a tear, Yeltsin even asked for the people's forgiveness
for the fact that "many of our dreams have not been realized."[31] Yeltsin per-
formed superbly in the last act of his spectacle, and he chose a good moment
for saying farewell to the nation, when it was relaxing, celebrating the New
Year, and ready to forgive him for all the unrealized dreams.

From a strictly formal point of view, the peaceful and voluntary resignation of the president, who had already long failed to meet his obligations,
could be judged positively. In any case, Russia succeeded in averting revolution, the holding on to the power of the Yeltsin corporation by force, or
the seizure of power by competing groups. But in fact the early departure
of Yeltsin and circumstances surrounding this move promoted the victory
of the successor he appointed, guaranteed the replication of the ruling corporation, and consequently narrowed the possibility of a democratic election for society. This example shows that pointing to only the formal signs
of Russian development, taking into account its "double low points," can
lead to an absolutely false sense of Russian reality. What is a confirmation

of the formation of "elected monarchy" can be perceived as proof of the presence of democracy.

Let us sum up and try to define the character of the leadership of Boris Yeltsin. First, which part of his legacy can be considered positive if we use liberal-democratic criteria? The consequence of Yeltsin's rule was the emergence, however spontaneous, of preconditions that make a return of Russia to communism impossible. Yeltsin himself and especially his reelection in 1996 put an end to the communist development of Russian society. At the same time, however, it was thanks to Yeltsin and his policies that the Communist Party in Russia still remains the most powerful political force in the country. Thanks to Yeltsin, democratic legitimization of power became the most important element of the political regime. He got the political elite accustomed to solving international questions in a relatively modern way, making a return to a cold war after the Yeltsin period more difficult, and perhaps impossible. To a large extent, Yeltsin guaranteed the peaceful breakup of the Soviet Union as well as the emergence on its territory of independent states. Under Yeltsin, a variety of interests in Russia also surfaced as he trained the political elite to exist in an atmosphere of pluralism and freedom of opinion. The course of events under Putin, however, suggests that the possibility remains that such trends could be reversed. Finally, Yeltsin made the return to a planned, centralized economy impossible.

But at the same time the negative aftermath of Yeltsin's rule should also be noted. It was under his government, with his perhaps unwitting participation, that corruption, shadowy relations, and the merger of political power and business became systemic, that is to say, stopped being random and temporary and turned into the most important component of survival for both the leader and society. Yeltsin returned Russia to the tradition of personalized rule. Finally, with his direct participation, there emerged in the country a regime that encouraged a lack of accountability in all political institutions, including the presidency. Under this regime, the parliament and the party do not feel responsible for the activities of the government that they failed to form. Having in his hands huge powers, the president did everything to avoid responsibility for the failures of his policies. It was under Yeltsin that the principles of liberal democracy were discredited, given that they were used as a façade for shady relations and autocratic rule.

Of course if you proceed from the fact that the number of tasks and challenges facing Russia was so huge and favorable circumstances for solving these problems on the path to liberal democracy were just as limited, then one could judge Yeltsin's actions less critically. But it should be noted that Yeltsin had several levers of power concentrated in his hands at the initial stage, when the political field and society had yet to be structured, and he had substantial opportunities to influence the course of events. Thus, there is no particular basis for justifying his weaknesses and failures. Consequently, it is Yeltsin who bears the responsibility for missed opportunities in carrying out reform, and therefore his leadership can hardly be summed up as positive. Even given all the obstacles, the country could have taken more decisive steps toward liberal democracy under a leader who made more consistent efforts to get beyond the limits of an autocratic and great-power model of development for Russia than did Yeltsin.

It is hard to accept the argument that Yeltsin should be judged less harshly since Russia avoided an apocalyptic scenario and no other strong contenders to the position of leader emerged under him. The fact that after Yeltsin's departure society began to aspire to a "firm hand" and turned toward more evident authoritarianism is by itself an unambiguous reflection on Yeltsin's government and his inability to affirm liberal-democratic values in society. Thus, if we proceed from a "passive" model of leadership oriented above all toward the maintenance of stability and stagnated development, then Yeltsin's leadership can even be said to be successful. But if we look to the needs of carrying out the democratic project and to the possibilities of doing so, of which there were many, then Yeltsin, of course, was a weak and inadequate leader.[32]

Yeltsin and his leadership were created out of unresolved conflicts. Formally possessing huge powers and at the same time powerless, he was incapable of carrying out his decisions. By nature prone to charismatic rule, he remained without mass support. A leader whose ideal was a presidential "vertical" power structure, he was compelled to act in a period of uncertainty and disintegration. A politician who hated compromise, he was forced to constantly make deals and concessions. Proclaiming the construction of democracy as his goal, he presided over the formation of autocracy. He won at democratic elections only to become a cover for clans that operated behind his back. Setting himself as an example of a person with a powerful and dynamic nature, he in fact constantly battled with depression.

Yeltsin turned out to be a revolutionary who managed to make revolutionary shock a means for his own survival. He became the destroyer of communism thanks to which the Communist Party nonetheless turned into a factor for his regime's survival. He became a leader under whom a significant part of society lost faith in democracy. However, there is one outcome of his leadership that, in my view, deserves approval: the weak, contradictory, chaotic leadership of Yeltsin trained society, or in any case a significant part of it, to think for itself, forced it to rely on its own strengths, and accustomed it to independence. And this fact alone, perhaps, will help Russia survive under any leader, which thus makes overcoming the country's traditional models of leadership easier. So, ironically, perhaps the main positive outcome of Boris Yeltsin's leadership lies in his weakness, indecisiveness, and insufficient firmness.

As for the price that Russia will have to pay for freeing itself from the tradition of autocracy, which was revived by Yeltsin, it will undoubtedly be very high. It is not now that Russia will have to pay the price, but in the future, when it becomes clear whether Putin succeeds in cleansing this autocracy of its chaotic nature and making it effective. If it turns out that he cannot, then society will be forced to pay for both the mistakes of the father of the regime and for those of his successor, who tried to make this regime work. It could turn out that the success of Yeltsin as a leader and reformer will be determined by how quickly his regime can be dismantled.

Let us make a paradoxical, even seditious, assumption: It cannot be ruled out that a shift of the Yeltsin regime on to a more severe authoritarian plane could turn out to be a blessing for Russia, for then the destructiveness of "elected monarchy," concealed democratic demagoguery, and pseudodemocratic façade would be exposed for all to see.

Yeltsin's Political Legacy in the Hands of His Successor

Dialectic of Vladimir Putin's Rise

Few in Russia or in the West believed that an obscure apparatchik from St. Petersburg with no experience in public policy appointed by Yeltsin as prime minister in August 1999 would have any political future. The chain of events in Russia proved that unexpected turns still might happen in this country.

The swift growth in popularity of a functionary who was unknown until recently and the lack of alternative candidates for the Russian presidency in the March 2000 elections are difficult to explain without taking account of the psychological atmosphere in Russian society between August and September 1999, when Vladimir Putin's rise began. His ascension coincided above all with a sharp increase in a large part of society of feelings of insecurity, personal defenselessness, and fear—a direct consequence of two events: the invasion of Chechen extremists in Dagestan, which led to large-scale military actions, and the explosions in apartment buildings in Moscow and several other Russian cities, resulting in the death of about 300 civilians.[33] Ever since, questions have remained unanswered: How did the Russian security forces allow for the concentration of fighters and their campaign in the neighboring republic, and who organized the explosions? The participation of Chechen fighters in these explosions has not been proved. But what is important is that these two events gave rise to mass support in Russian society for a strong leader and order. The "antiterrorist operation" begun by Vladimir Putin allowed him to demonstrate that he could respond firmly to growing fears.[34] Moreover, the use of the Chechen war and the search for an enemy against which to rally society and consolidate the regime dictated from the very beginning a certain logic of the new authorities, making them more dependent on security structures and the return of the country, however partially, to the way of thinking in Soviet times. The very appearance of the demand for a regime with an authoritarian leader shows the unstable mood of society and rootless democratic views as well as the susceptibility of a large part of the population to manipulation by the authorities. In the course of a rather short period, a wide section of Russian citizens sharply changed their political orientation. Even as recently as summer 1999, the most popular political leader was former prime minister Yevgeny Primakov who embodied a rather moderate, careful bureaucratic leadership. But, very quickly, by the fall of that same year, under the influence of the above-mentioned events, the strict leadership of the previously obscure Putin came to the fore.[35]

An equally significant reason for the rise of Putin is the fact that the majority of the population saw him ironically as both the chosen successor of the outgoing president and an alternative or even antithesis to him. Putin offered the opportunity for a more dynamic leader than Yeltsin; yet, for many Russians, it was important that this alternative had been proposed officially by the authorities, indeed by Yeltsin himself, and was not part of some nonsystemic plan of the opposition. This felt need for the approval of the existing order shows that Russian society on the whole is still not used to thinking in the ways of opposition politics and is not ready to acknowledge the right of the opposition to exercise real power. In the thinking of most people, the opposition only has the right to put forward a theoretical alternative and to criticize the authorities.

Many people still consider that simply trying to improve upon the policies of the authorities is the optimal solution for Russia, which shows that they still look on power as a substance that reproduces itself rather than arises from society. The fact that ordinary citizens and the political elite calmly accepted the nomination of Putin as Yeltsin's successor and that very few were troubled by the almost complete absence of alternative candidates shows that society still relates to power in a semi-monarchistic way. In short, in the public thinking, Putin embodied a connection with the past, which the people did not like but from which they were not yet ready to dissociate themselves, and at the same time a negation of this past.

Putin's lack of a political biography and clear political preferences— which made him, in effect, a "blank slate"—also played a role in helping him gain popularity and support. In a developed and well-structured society, the lack of political experience on the part of a candidate for the highest office would be considered a handicap. In Russia, the opposite is true. Putin's lack of a political past was a big plus, giving various groups and forces the opportunity to hope that they could coopt the new leader and win him over to their side. Putin's lack of party affiliation and clear political views helped him build, at an early stage, a rather wide social and political foundation. It was only natural that he tried to avoid giving concrete responses to questions about his plans before the elections. This lack of specificity was a way of preserving his broad political base, made up of supporters with extremely diverse orientations from liberals to great-state advocates to leftists.

The morally repressive consciousness that still exists at all levels of Russian society also played a significant role in Putin's rise. Those at the top saw Putin as a leader who could help them keep their property, which they had acquired under Yeltsin, and ensure their safety in case of possible social unrest. Those at the bottom saw Putin as a politician who would protect them against the oligarchs and the bureaucracy and guarantee their poor but safe existence. It is the morally repressive consciousness that requires a "firm hand" and an authoritarian, or possibly dictatorial, regime. And it was this consciousness that promoted Putin's rise.

Putin's coming to power also illuminates a shift in the type of political leadership that can be accepted, largely due to the influence of the exemplars of the new Russia. People had lost faith in the traditional type of leader who had come from a village or a province and was elderly, conservative, experienced in bureaucratic struggle, and represented the Soviet *nomenklatura*. For the first time in Russian history, the leader was a relatively young, educated, and urban individual who came from the old capital of St. Petersburg and who had lived abroad and spoke a foreign language. The contrast between Putin and Yeltsin is striking: the new Russian leader, or at least a leader with a new kind of personality, is the exact opposite of the first Russian president. Putin's appearance on the scene and the support he received showed that the need to get away from a revolutionary cycle and make a transition to a stable environment required a new type of leader.

That Putin is not a charismatic figure or a bright personality also played in his favor. He is an unprepossessing person, "just like everyone else," whose appearance and behavior make him almost a man on the street and allowed many Russians to identify themselves with the new leader. Everything about him—beginning with his biography, his origins in the KGB, which society considers the least corrupted organization,[36] and ending with his clothes, appearance, modesty, dullness, sportsman style, and ability to use street slang—impressed a wide section of Russian citizens, who had grown tired of Yeltsin's colorful personality and imposing nature and of the talkativeness of other leaders. Putin's lack of charisma and public presence and his reserve, even asceticism, helped his rise to power. Whether these qualities will help him hold on to power is still an open question.

A portrait of the new president's leadership can be drawn from some of the traits that emerged when he began forming his government. On the one hand, this was a person who was clearly interested in normalizing relations with the West and was already accustomed to working under conditions of a market economy. But on the other hand, he could not be what he did not understand. Rather, he proved to be suspicious of the main elements of political democracy—freedom of the press,[37] freedom of the opposition, and competition in politics. He saw no special need to seek torturous compromises with separate political forces, but preferred to rule through the state apparatus. His policies in Chechnya and attempts to gain a victory or the appearance of victory by any means, regardless of the bloodletting and clear sign of a dead-end situation, could not but raise some misgivings. Furthermore, Putin's behavior before the presidential election was clearly not designed to encourage popular participation in determining Russia's future direction, for he categorically refused to explain his program. "I won't say," he announced, in response to a question about his plans.[38] It was as if Putin were saying to the people: "I won't tell you a thing, and that's the way you'll vote for me. Where else can you go?"[39] This tactic, however, turned out to be successful, for it helped Putin maintain his ambiguous image, and therefore the rather extensive and unstructured basis of popular support, and at the same time eliminate the problem of being held accountable for his election campaign promises.

A final important factor that aided Putin's ascendancy to power was the December 1999 parliamentary campaign. The Kremlin succeeded in inventing a new "party of power," the Unity party, which was completely dependent on the Kremlin for financial resources and which won 23 percent of the popular vote on the party list. When the Unity party defeated the Fatherland-All Russia movement, the electoral block headed by Yevgeny Primakov and Moscow Mayor Yury Luzhkov, it thus ended all chances for Primakov's presidential bid. Parliamentary elections therefore became both amazingly successful primaries for Putin and a way to undermine all his potential rivals.[40] In addition, during the parliamentary election, the Kremlin experimented with new manipulation "technologies" and mud-slinging techniques which later were used to intimidate Putin's opponents and consolidate his base.

Putin had been provided with no other option than to gain an indisputable victory in March 2000, thanks to the fact that he succeeded in receiving the support of those who were interested in stability as well as those interested in renewal.[41]

Putin Dismantles the Yeltsin Regime

It was already clear by May or June 2000 that Vladimir Putin understood the logic of survival behind the formation of the Yeltsin regime: in order for the regime to be maintained, a successor must be named. But for the successor to be legitimate and capable of governing independently, he would have to renounce succession or his part in it and try not only to build his own support but also to change the functioning of power mechanisms. For the sake of his own survival, Putin was forced to shift from his role as Yeltsin's successor to the role of a destroyer of the Yeltsin regime, and what he began to do is entirely in keeping with the concept of an anti-Yeltsin revolution.[42] Thus, while he was still in power, Yeltsin himself, whether wittingly or not does not matter, was forced to search for a formula of uniting succession with its very negation.

The new president apparently set himself the task of combining two kinds of development—mobilization in politics and innovation in the economy. This task signaled a move away from the flexibility and tolerance of the Yeltsin government and toward a more rigid form of leadership. It seems that Putin at first tried to balance this task by postponing structural economic reform until he controlled all the levers of power. He began his presidency by dismantling the basic principles of the Yeltsin political regime, while preserving the formula for "elected monarchy." Instead of Yeltsin's principle of mutual connivance, Putin began to introduce the principles of discipline and subordination. Instead of the Yeltsin system of shadowy checks and balances, with its horizontal ties, Putin started to build a "transmission belt" system, based on strict vertical subordination. He renounced anticommunism and began to exercise a pragmatic style of leadership, demonstrating a readiness to rely on very diverse forces and avoiding permanent alliances and party support. In the framework of his new pragmatism, he was entirely prepared to make compromises with the Communist Party.

If Yeltsin was forced to rely on favorites and oligarchs, then Putin at the beginning of his presidency made it clear that he had decided to make a clean break with old interest groups and began an "anti-oligarchic revolution." He cast his lot with the bureaucracy and security structures, thus changing not only the balance of forces on the political field but also the very base of support for his regime. If Yeltsin largely avoided bringing representatives of the security structures into the formal political process, then Putin began to openly grant power to representatives of the special services and the prosecutors.[43] If Yeltsin held on to power at the expense of its redistribution and fragmentation, then Putin attempted to consolidate power, return it to the center while limiting the powers of regional and other elites, and begin the process of restructuring an asymmetrical federation and lending it a unitary character. If Yeltsin permitted several political freedoms, including political pluralism and freedom of the press, then Putin began to move in the direction of "regulated democracy," limiting the independence of other political freedoms. In short, the direction of the evolution of the Yeltsin regime under Putin became clearly toward more authoritarian rule, which the president himself for some reason called "civilized liberalism," apparently understanding the Yeltsin rule as "uncivilized liberalism." Thus, although the first stage of Putin's rule looked rather revolutionary, it remained to be seen to what extent he was devoted to dismantling Yeltsin's logic and whether he could offer both the people and the ruling class a different type of rule.

Further events from the end of 2000 through the beginning of 2001 demonstrated that Putin continues to contemplate what kind of power he wants to build. But the way he thinks about power is worth noting. In response to a question of whether restoring the monarchy in Russia is worth considering, Putin said: "On the whole . . . in certain periods of time . . . in a certain place . . . in certain conditions the monarchy has played and plays to this day a positive role. . . . The monarch does not have to think about whether he will be elected or not, make petty conjectures, somehow influence the electorate. He can think about the fate of his people, and not be distracted by trifles."[44] "But in Russia that is impossible," journalists told Putin. "You know," he answered, "much appears to us as impossible and unrealizable, and then—bang! As it was with the Soviet Union. Who could have imagined that it would take it upon itself and collapse." This passage speaks to the fact that the new Russian president is in no way excluding a movement of Russia this time toward unambiguous monarchy.

So the question inevitably arises: What kind of regime will Putin build in the end?

To judge by external signs, in only a short period the new president has accomplished a lot. He neutralized the regional bosses and oligarchic groups. He managed to get in his pocket the Federation Council, which previously was a counterweight to presidential authority. He forced the Duma to renounce confrontation and got it to collaborate with him by leaning for support on his loyal faction. Furthermore, in order to strengthen his rule, Putin relies on the pro-presidential factions of Unity, People's Deputy, and the Communist Party. And when he must introduce market laws, he turns for support to the right-wing Union of Rightist Forces and Yabloko. Yeltsin never had such a favorable atmosphere. By the end of 2000, there remained no rivals or serious competitors for Putin on the political scene. Moreover, he had succeeded in concentrating control in his hands over all the administrative and financial levers of state, which under Yeltsin were controlled by various interest groups. All this seems to create good opportunities for him to further strengthen his power and form a bridgehead for winning the presidential elections in 2004.

Nonetheless, the victory march of the new president and his honeymoon with the people became clouded by the drama of the sunken submarine *Kursk* in August 2000. Events surrounding this drama demonstrated Putin's lack of confidence as a leader, his inexperience, his reluctance to make out-of-the-ordinary decisions, and, most important, his lack of intuition and feeling, which is particularly important for a leader in Russia. Putin's ratings in August 2000 fell from 73 percent to 60 percent, which for him was a palpable blow.[45] The August drama itself, in which one crisis followed another (the explosion in the center of Moscow, the fire in the Ostankino television broadcasting tower), demonstrated that Putin, who came to power under auspicious circumstances, was not yet ready to manage crises. It is still unclear whether he has enough time to assimilate this experience. But most important, the events of August showed that the new president lacks the intuition to gauge the mood of society and sense its turning points, which in Russia can in no way be measured and is often difficult to explain. Yeltsin, it should be said, did have these qualities; they formed the basis of his leadership. Neither experience nor knowledge can compensate for a lack of this intuition.

Moreover, early in 2001, it was revealed that despite all the efforts at unifying the political scene, the new ruling team could not fully govern on the basis of subordination and, in the last analysis, it was gradually forced to return to elements typical of Yeltsin's system of haggling and political barter. The essence of this system is loyalty to the leader on the part of certain social and political groups in exchange for his toleration and a certain freedom of action. After a very brief period of scare tactics and harsh announcements about establishing order, the Kremlin was forced to resort to compromises with the oligarchs, regional bosses, and certain other groups (liberals, communists, etc.). True, it should be noted that Putin's policy of compromises and bargaining is still limited. Unlike Yeltsin, who often became hostage to the arrangements he made, Putin controls the situation and, in all his compromises, at least for the time being, maintains a dominant role.

The policy of compromise and permissiveness that the Kremlin has begun to implement includes a conscious effort to balance the influence of separate political forces and avoid relying exclusively on any one of them. Thus the ruling team made deals with the communists when it allotted them several leading posts in the Duma. But the Kremlin soon supported the liberal version of tax law, thereby making a step toward the liberals. At the same time, by making belligerent declarations concerning Chechnya and employing great-power rhetoric toward the West, the ruling team was able to fully neutralize the nationalists and great-power advocates.

The easing of the "transmission belt" system can be explained above all by the ruling team's conclusion that the central authorities' resources are limited and it is impossible to implement a policy of subordination without strengthening the policy of force. But there is a lot of evidence that Putin, at least at the moment, was not prepared to turn to severe and explicit force. Apparently, the central authorities have realized that scare tactics bring only partial results. In short, the ruling team seems to have concluded that constructing the entire political scene along vertical lines combined with a straightforward policy of pressure is not sufficiently effective. Instead it began to return to the policy, already tested by Yeltsin, of "everyone gets what is coming to him," that is, partial satisfaction of various forces, albeit while maintaining the same severe and often openly authoritarian rhetoric. When Putin felt threatened, however, he could go beyond rhetoric and strike a blow as he did when he cracked down on the media empire of Gusinsky in spring of 2001.

In this context, let us examine all the factors that, on the one hand, will help Putin's leadership during the consolidation of his regime and, on the other, will make it more difficult. Among the favorable factors is unquestionably the economic situation, which is characterized by economic growth, low inflation, and a stabilizing standard of living. But it should not be forgotten that these successes have been based largely on the high price of oil, not on successful structural reform. Putin's leadership is also helped by the fragmentation of the political elite and society itself, as well as the lack of leadership alternatives and absence of a united opposition to the economic course. The absence of alternatives and opposition signifies the weakening of democratic forces and their inability to put forward an influential leader who could confront Putin. What is even more significant is the people's disillusion with previous reforms, the increased conservatism of part of the population, and a popular notion of democracy as synonymous with chaos and disorder. The orientation toward survival at any cost, including the price of lowering the ceiling of aspirations and hopes, also plays a role. Curiously, more than a year after Putin came to power, his approval ratings have remained high, but the expectations for his rule are substantially lower. In October 2000, he was supported by 64 percent of those polled. But in April 2000, 55 percent of those polled thought the economic situation in Russia had improved, whereas in September only 38 percent believed this to be true. In April 2000, 47 percent believed that the situation with rights and freedoms would improve, whereas in September only 23 percent of those polled thought this way. In October 2000, only 28 percent of respondents thought that Russia was moving in the right direction, and 52 percent believed that "events would lead us into a dead end."[46] In April 2001, Putin's approval rating remained high: he was supported by 71 percent of respondents (only 20 percent of those polled disapproved), though only 10 percent thought that he keeps his promises.[47]

Against this background, how can the president's high ratings be explained? The main reason lies in the lack of an alternative to Putin and concern that a new fight for power would only make matters worse. But although Putin's lack of rivals or competitors remains the main reason for his popularity, many continue to wait for him to establish the kind of "order" that would match their aspirations.

Now let us turn to the obstacles and restraints with which Putin has already clashed or will inevitably collide. An unquestionable obstacle would be the emergence of powerful interest groups. Despite the outward meekness of both the regional elite and the oligarchic groups (with the exception of several oligarchs such as Boris Berezovsky and Vladimir Gusinsky), the central authorities will hardly be able to destroy the independent interest groups that are capable of sabotaging the Kremlin's policies. But even the loyalty of the main elite groups are not really a gift to Putin: the servility of the political elite, as the history of Russia has shown, quickly leads to the degradation of the government and irresponsibility of the ruling class. Moreover, the lack of lively discussion over options for development, the weakening of open opposition activities, which are being driven under deeper and deeper, and the appearance of fear of the authorities, which had disappeared under Gorbachev and Yeltsin—all of this is capable of creating destructive forces that will seek to resolve their concerns by circumventing official channels.

An even more substantial factor is the fact that Putin's policies are still apparently linked to the forces that helped him take power and therefore obligate him to grant them favors.[48] Furthermore, the exceptions to the rule make the establishment of a strict "vertical" structure of power based on a pure authoritarian "transmission belt" impossible. Moreover, for the sake of maintaining his base of power and support in society, Putin still must not make his image concrete. Consequently, he is obliged to keep groups with varying aspirations and ideologies as his base of support—from advocates of a strong state to liberals. The example of this "everybody's man" policy was offered by Putin in a package of new Russian state symbols that even included the Soviet anthem approved by Stalin. The new symbols that were supposed to satisfy all major groups instead revived old conflicts and animosity and weakened the president's support within the democratic community. Thus, instead of consolidation, the policy of being "everything for everybody" created the impression that the leader lacks a sense of direction and tries hard to preserve stability and the status quo at any cost. Besides, the attempt to be everything for everybody in the end might make the leader appear weak and disoriented.

It could be that a transition to subordination and the ideology of order will force Putin to be more explicit and unambiguous. Sooner or later, he will have to define himself—regarding the question of Yeltsin's legacy and the oligarchs, as well as the question of the future of the federation and Russia's role in the world. Remaining amorphous and undefined could cause him to lose his image as a politician who knows what to do and has a clear vision of the future of Russia. Becoming more unequivocal, however, could deprive him of wide support in society and stimulate the emergence of an opposition either among supporters of a powerful state and leftists or liberals and Westernizers.

It is particularly worth noting that Putin gained the support of the people not because of attractive programs or concrete political activities, but due to the artificial inflation of his approval ratings, his populism, and his successfully playing on the deep fears of the population. In the final analysis, he turned out to be hostage to these factors as well as to his ratings and the team that helped provide them by manipulating popular opinion. What came of this? He was forced to look for quick solutions and take populist steps without considering their consequences. Being hostage to the "technology of success" narrows the scope of his reformist, but potentially unpopular actions.

Even more significant is the trap in which Putin will be caught if he continues his attempts to maintain control over all the levers of power. In fact, in the absence of a division of responsibilities among institutions, with complete concentration of power in the hands of a single leader, he will be held accountable for all blunders and mistakes at both the federal and local levels. This situation will lead to local powers' making mistakes under the cover of the president and to the president's gradually losing his legitimacy—the main systemic trap of the regime in which Putin could be caught.

Moreover, the regime's weakened democratic beginnings, which were necessary to make it legitimate, had to be filled in by strengthening its coercive foundations. But the question arises whether the state has enough resources to consolidate society through coercion. Such a consolidation requires at least three factors: a well-paid army that enjoys a high status, a monolithic and effective bureaucracy, and the consent of society to consolidation through coercive means. Today the central authorities are facing conflicts within the army that are demoralizing it and tearing it apart; the security structures are at odds with one another; and the bureaucracy is divisive and corrupt. As for society, despite the apparent support for the idea of a "firm hand," the Russian people could turn out to be unwilling to lose the freedoms to which they have become accustomed. Almost half of the respondents at the end of 2000 believed that Russia needs a strong opposition to Putin; only 29 percent thought such an opposition was unnecessary. Fifty-three percent thought that an independent media was a necessary part of society, while 27 percent did not. Only 36 percent of respondents were prepared to limit their freedoms and democracy for the sake of strengthening Russia's state power; 52 percent were categorically against such limits. In April 2001, after the state took over independent national television channel NTV, 53 percent of respondents were in favor of political pluralism and freedom of the media and 43 percent disapproved of the crackdown on NTV, while 41 percent thought it was a legitimate action aimed to resolve the financial dispute.[49] This support for freedoms would make it difficult for Russia to return to an authoritarian or quasi-authoritarian type of leadership, which would require mobilizing the country, even if Putin suddenly turned to pure coercion. If the democratic legitimacy of the authorities becomes weakened and there are not enough means of coercion to mobilize the country, then the leader will invariably turn out to be powerless and lose his former firmness.

Putin's Dilemmas

At the start of 2001, Putin was faced with a dilemma: introducing innovative models for transforming the economy, that is, decisive structural reforms, which Yeltsin was incapable of accomplishing, would mean destroying the basis for the relative stability in society—patron-client relations. But if this were to happen, the president would face losing the support of many groups that exist because of shadowy relations and that see him as a guarantor of their well-being. The result would shatter stability in society. Is Putin ready to do this? At this particular stage, it was not clear.

Furthermore, he was not even able during this time to consolidate his base of support to effect decisive structural reforms.

Putin's policies still leave the impression that he is trying to base his power and economic measures on the principle of personal loyalty. This is reflected in his allowing separate groups of influence to operate in a "gray zone," permitting them to circumvent the law if they are personally loyal to him. This selective approach is unlikely to help him make effective reforms, one of the goals of which is to eliminate the union between political power and business. For now at least, Putin himself is trying to change the nature of this union and make business dependent on the state and the leader. But the patron-client relations that have developed remain unchanged and could undermine the future course of reform.

Theoretically, it cannot be ruled out that Putin will pursue more vigorously the idea of a "transmission belt" system, will overcome his hesitation, and will take more decisive steps toward making his regime more authoritarian—first by neutralizing independent political actors and curbing political freedoms. As Putin said in an interview with French journalists before his visit to Paris in October 2000: "The state has in its hands a cudgel that strikes only once. But on the head. We have not yet resorted to this cudgel. We have simply laid our hands on it, and this turned out to be enough to attract attention. But if we are angered, we won't hesitate to put it to use."[50] This statement can be considered a manifesto of the new post-Yeltsin authorities. It points to the direction in which Putin still is trying to move, emphasizing the bureaucratic-coercive component of his regime. But the question remains: Will simple solutions help unravel the very complex knot of Russian development?

There is much more evidence that Putin's leadership is most likely to evolve with attempts to consolidate his regime through a mixture of semi-authoritarian steps and political bargaining. What does this entail? It means the tactic of "one step forward, one step back." The president will continue to increase control over all institutions, influence the formation of parties friendly to the Kremlin, strengthen control over the news media, and create his own loyal oligarchs. But if this policy of building a manageable political field meets resistance, he will most likely temporarily yield and even step back. Such a "policy of impulses" could include the wide use of means of fear and manipulation. But the fact is that the politics of fear can only be partially effective, since the failure to strike a coercive blow—that is, apply force—could create the impression that the authorities are powerless.

Manipulative politics also have their limits. As the experience of Putin's rise has shown, the manipulative use of technology to exclude opponents and boost the president's ratings can only be successful during elections. But in the process of real governing, virtual means of supporting the president gradually lose their significance. What is needed are concrete and palpable results from his actions. In the end, the policy of "one step forward, one step back" will most likely produce only the imitation of a strong state and effective leadership. As a result of the evolution of Yeltsin's political legacy under Putin, we can ascertain the formation in Russia of a hybrid bureaucratic quasi-authoritarian regime which at the moment is not stable or consolidated and can develop in different directions. This regime, less patrimonial and seemingly more rational and pragmatic than Yeltsin's, fully fits within the framework of Yeltsin's "elected monarchy." That is, the very formal and constitutional basis for the structure of the Yeltsin regime remains as before, comprising a personal style of governing and a concentration of all the levers of power and administration in the hands of the president, with a weak role reserved for other institutions and the same merger of power and capital. Still, because the other sources of legitimacy of power in present-day Russia—the armed forces, parties, ideology, hereditary monarchy—have become exhausted, the need for exercising democratic institutions, above all elections, to legitimize this power most likely will be preserved, but their democratic substance will become thin.

As for possible steps Putin will take regarding the economy, it is clear that if he does not use his high ratings and the favorable economic conditions for conducting more decisive reforms (such as adopting the second part of the tax code, land reform, judicial reform, bank reform, and guarantees of private property), then it is possible he will not be able to accomplish them by the end of his term.

In spring 2001, Putin pushed forward the implementation of long-delayed judicial, pension, housing, and utility reforms. He initiated the change of leadership in Gazprom. The office of General Prosecutor reopened investigation into the activity of some influential members of Yeltsin's "family," including notorious oligarch Roman Abramovich, which could not happen without the consent of the Kremlin. These steps gave rise to hopes that Putin had finally begun his liberal breakthrough. But so far, a lot of questions remain. It is unclear whether the ruling team will succeed with painful reforms that exclude the public from dialogue on their substance. It is also not clear if Putin's reshuffles and distancing from the previous entourage demonstrate readiness to change the interdependence between political power and business or if it simply means a changing of the guard and an attempt to expand his own constituency. So far there are no answers. As long as the Russian president continues to rely upon personal networks and the loyalty of his own cadres, and until he is willing to go beyond making governance *look* more rational and pragmatic and actually changes its substance, he hardly can change the previous logic of development. In the final analysis, he might only become a hostage of the surrogate, imitation democracy that has emerged in Russia.

If Putin fails to break the logic of personal networking, it cannot be ruled out that he will be forced to return to a policy of connivance and pay for his survival with concessions to interest groups. But no one would be able to guarantee his survival, for the political elite, which is accustomed to changing its allegiance at will, can at any moment support a new pretender to the role of master of the Kremlin, if this claimant offers a more advantageous deal.

Boris Berezovsky, who bears much responsibility for the degradation of power in Russia and for the changes now occurring in the country, should be quoted in this regard. Having been thrown out of the circle of power, the observant Berezovsky was able to give a good diagnosis of the policies that the Kremlin is now trying to carry out. "Putin," he says, "does not believe that Russia is ready to become a liberal, free country. He does believe that the president or other bosses should still take care of people."[51]

This paternalism and attempt of the new team to make the people happy and punish heterodox thinkers—although for the time being not yet severely, but simply by scolding and threatening with the finger—have already begun to bear fruit. Some Russian citizens have preserved the remnants of slavery, and some have even taken refuge in the Soviet past with pleasure. Some have begun to glorify Putin enthusiastically, others have started to write textbooks about him, yet others have created for him political parties and youth organizations. Part of the country has begun to return to a seemingly forgotten time. There are some signs, however, of a degree of optimism, largely among thinking people who are accustomed to analyzing events independently and for whom a return to lack of freedom would be very difficult, if not impossible. According to opinion polls, such thinking people in Russian society make up between 44 and 47 percent of the population including about 15 percent of Westernizers, those who consider liberal democracy and moving Russia toward Europe the optimal scenario. For the moment, a good number of them are still biding their time, giving Putin a chance, and even agreeing to some limits on their freedom for the sake of market reform. But this part of the population clearly does not wish to live in a society that operates on the principle of a "transmission belt," and sooner or later it will present a serious problem for the new team if that team continues on its course of turning society into a marching colony.

Putin will apparently have to dispel several illusions linked to reform of Yeltsin's government. First is the illusion of a relatively painless construction of a presidential "pyramid" in a pluralistic society accustomed to freedom. He will have to think about how to make his authority legitimate, given the lack of independent institutions in the country other than the presidency, and how under such conditions he can avoid responsibility for the failures of those at every level of power who become appendages of the presidency.

The hope that the president's strength will help to continue economic reform could also turn out to be an illusion. Few remember that, in 1991, Yeltsin tried to introduce liberal authoritarianism in Russia, but nothing came of it. Today apologists of the new "firm hand" in Russia try to show that Yeltsin was unable to accomplish anything because of his weakness and inconsistency. Putin, they argue, will have more luck because he is a disciplined person and knows how to apply coercive methods. As for the many cases in world history of failed attempts to make authoritarian and totalitarian regimes economically effective, the Russian ruling team is not so far interested in drawing analogies. Yet again, there are powerful groups in Russia who try to force society to start a new experiment on its own only to convince itself of its more than likely failure.

An "elected monarchy" based on the loyalty of cadres to a single figure and their servility—a mere imitation of democratic institutions—could turn out to be a form of strengthening shadowy relations and corruption. In any case, the regime's reliance on the bureaucracy, which in Russia has long been the coffin maker of any reform, will hardly promote economic transformations. It is rather more likely that something else will occur: given the lack of counterbalances, the bureaucracy could make the president its hostage. In addition, by bringing representatives of the security structures and especially the secret service into the government, its closed nature and opaque decision making process will only be exacerbated, which will make dominating the narrow interests groups within it easier.

Thus there are serious doubts about whether the attempt of Vladimir Putin to unite mobilizing and innovative types of development as well as find a formula for a dynamic leadership based on the subordination and loyalty of cadres can be effective. Moreover, there are doubts about whether such an attempt can be carried out at all. It is rather likely that Putin's idea of a vertical and coordinated pyramidal structure of power will fail in the end. So far, Putin has discovered increased uneasiness to make decisions and tried to escape taking responsibility, demonstrating a lack of sense of direction, thus proving that he most probably is not a candidate for the role of a Russian Pinochet. But it is still unclear what Putin will do, when he fails to create a "transmission belt" in contemporary Russia: will he allow independent institutions to operate and grow and renounce autocracy and personified rule; or, out of frustration, will he try to establish a regime with a firm rule; or will he continue his policy of avoiding the final choice? Only time will provide answers to these questions.

The future of Putin's leadership will depend a lot on his capacity for evolution—for acquiring the skills of a politician, for understanding the many directions in which society will develop, and for recognizing the need for social consensus on the basic questions of Russia's development. The dynamism and pragmatism of Putin and his striving to understand complex phenomena give some hope for his ability to expand on his political experience. It seems that the international community still has many opportunities for influencing him.

At the same time the character of the negative circumstances, from a liberal-democratic perspective, that in the near future will influence the Russian president should be taken into account. Among them is the lack of powerful democratic forces that would attempt to reform the elected autocracy. But even more serious is that all the main participants in the political process are accustomed to stability through shadowy relations, which form a systemic element that has saturated not only the economy but also Russian politics, and into which society itself has been drawn. It appears that Putin is hoping that, having accumulated all the resources of power and eliminated all the centers of influence, he will be able to take steps toward more decisive market reform. But it should be recalled that, when Yeltsin was formulating his leadership, he tried to do the same and ended up trading away his power for the sake of self-preservation as well as causing the degradation and decay of his regime.

Putin has, albeit theoretically, the chance to make a breakthrough. But he is left with little time to do so, and the steps he has already taken are leading Russia to new disappointments, for which some price will have to be paid. Thus, the result of the latest experiment of trying to prolong the life of autocracy in the 21st century is almost clear. What is uncertain is in which direction Russia will go when it becomes clear that the resources of autocratic forms of leadership have been exhausted.

Notes

1. Boris Yeltsin, *Zapiski prezidenta* (Moscow, 1994), p. 14. (Available in English as *The Struggle for Russia,* trans. Catherine A. Fitzpatrick [New York: Times Books, 1994].)

2. Ibid., p. 14.

3. Ibid., p. 153.

4. Yeltsin not only used force in 1993 to dissolve the Parliament, but he also considered refusing to hold presidential elections in 1996. As he himself acknowledges in his memoirs, he even prepared a decree on postponing these elections. See Boris Yeltsin, *Prezidentskiy marafon* (Moscow: ACT, 2000), pp. 31–33. (Available in English as *Midnight Diaries,* trans. Catherine A. Fitzpatrick [New York: Public Affairs, 2000].)

5. One of the then-leaders of the democrats, Gavriil Popov, remarked that the democrats expected only one thing from Yeltsin: posts in the government. "Some already occupied posts, others expected them, and still others requested them," wrote Popov. Gavriil Popov, *Snova v oppozitsii* (Moscow: Galaktika, 1994), p. 264.

6. It is for this reason that events often caught Yeltsin unaware. Thus, despite his long period of struggle with Mikhail Gorbachev, after the attempted coup in August 1991, Yeltsin turned out to be completely unprepared to exercise the power that had fallen at his feet. Neither he nor his team had any plan for a new government structure, provisions for staffing it, or a clear strategy for economic reform.

7. Yeltsin, *Zapiski prezidenta,* p. 347.

8. Ibid., p. 311.

9. The essence of Yeltsin's political nature and his relationship to politics was reflected well in his memoirs, *The Struggle for Russia* and *Midnight Diaries.* We will not find here reflections of the president of a new Russia on the tormenting problems of building a new government, on the hierarchy of values, and on the contours of the future Russia. Both books are a confirmation of Yeltsin's interest in only one problem: shakeups of government posts and court politics.

10. Michael McFaul was right when he wrote: "They [Yeltsin and his team] had to tackle the problems of empire, economic reform and political change with many of the practices and institutions still in place." "Yeltsin's Legacy," *Wilson Quarterly,* Spring 2000, p. 47.

11. Officially 57.1 percent of the electorate voted for the new constitution and 41.6 percent against. In fact, it was supported by about 31 percent of Russian voters. However, according to the conclusions of independent investigators, the real participation of citizens in the vote was less than 50 percent. The rest were made up of additions. Thus, the constitution was hardly approved by the population. See Lilia Shevtsova, *Rezhim Borisa Yel'tsina* (Moscow: Moscow Carnegie Center, 1999), p. 153.

12. Lev Tikhomirov, *Monarkhicheskaya gosudarstvennost'* (Moscow: Alir, 1998).

13. Fareed Zakaria. "The Rise of Illiberal Democracy," *Foreign Affairs* 76, no. 6 (1997): 39.

14. See A. Panarin, *Revansh istorii: rossiyskaia strategicheskaya initsiativa v XXI veke* (Moscow, 1998).

15. Igor Klyamkin and Lilia Shevtsova, *Vnesistemnyy rezhim Borisa Vtorogo. Nekotorye osobennosti politicheskogo razvitiya postsovetskoy Rossii* (Moscow: Moscow Carnegie Center, 1999), pp. 40–41.

16. To define the Yeltsin regime it is useful to borrow the terms that Philippe C. Schmitter and Terry Lynn Karl used to describe other hybrid regimes—the Spanish neologisms "democradura," a civilian government controlled by military and authoritarian elements, "dictablanda," or "tutelary democracy"—as well as Guillermo O'Donnell's "delegative democracy," Richard Sakwa's "authoritarian democracy," the "electoral democracy" of, among others, Michael McFaul, and the "illiberal democracy" of Fareed Zakaria. These definitions allow us to make certain progress in understanding the essence of the Yeltsin regime. However, these definitions still do not fully convey the particularities of the Russian regime, in which outwardly incompatible monarchical powers and ways of ruling are combined with democratic mechanisms of legitimating authority.

17. My coauthor, Igor Klyamkin, and I wrote in this regard: "If the form of rule, which had a place in Russia in 1906–1917, could be called a constitutionally succession-based monarchy, then Russia can rightly be called today a constitutionally elected monarchy. This, of course, does not mean that the powers invested in the Russian president are the same as those of the Russian emperor (although on the federal level they are entirely comparable to the imperial powers of the Duma period). The proposed term puts the present authorities in Russia in a national historical context and reflects the inheritance, although in diminished form, of its specificity." Klyamkin and Shevtsova, p. 41.

18. The role of Yeltsin as a constitutional monarch was not identical to the role of the "republican monarch" that the former French prime minister Michel Debré described when he was preparing a new constitution for de Gaulle. For the French elected monarch, de Gaulle, still acted under conditions of the existence of a rather influential parliament and strong cabinet. See Ezra N. Suleiman, "Presidential Government in France," in *Presidents and Prime Ministers,* ed. Richard Rose and Ezra Suleiman (Washington, D.C.: American Enterprise Institute for Public Research, 1980), pp. 94–97.

19. At the time when Europe was experiencing social revolutions, the beginning of the rise of the nation-state, and the restructuring of authority between the sixteenth and seventeenth centuries, independent individuals started to form; sixteenth-century Russia, on the contrary, had its own revolution, during which autocratic power that swallowed society and the individual arose. See Yu. Pivovarov and A. Fursov, "Russkaia vlast? Istoriya i sovremennost'," *Politiya* no. 1 (Spring 1999): 79.

20. A. Fursov and Yu. Pivovarov wrote in this connection: "Russia, in essence, intuitively seeks forms and frameworks that greatly resemble those that existed before 1917. Thus, in the Constitution of December 17, 1993 it is not hard to reveal the traits that are characteristic for the political-legal building of this country in the period of 1906–1917, which in turn were formed beginning with the reform of M. M. Speransky. Of course, this is not a mere coincidence. Here culture is trying to obtain the configuration and the order to which they were aspiring in the course of centuries." "Pravopreemstvo i russkaya vlast'," *Politiya* no. 1 (1998): 71. M. Il'in also wrote about this: "Russia is once again defining itself politically as oriented

toward modernization of autocracy, with the only difference being that this time it is masked by quasi-democratic rhetoric." "Politicheskoe samoopredelenie Rossii," *Pro et Contra,* Summer 1999, p. 83.

21. See Il'in, "Politicheskoe samoopredelenie Rossii," p. 74.

22. The ideological bloc did not succeed in being restored under Yeltsin, although Yeltsin's team did try for a long time to come up with a new "national idea" for Russia. Under Putin's rule attempts to restore an ideocratic bloc were renewed—this involved finding a new basis for the idea of a great power while taking into account Russia's limited possibilities.

23. One of the interesting, though controversial attempts to define the character of the Yeltsin regime is the research carried out by Richard Sakwa, which introduced the definition of the "regime system." While not agreeing with his understanding of the systemic nature of the Yeltsin regime, I fully support his view of what constituted the essential characteristics of this regime. Sakwa wrote: "The regime system embodied elements of continuity but also inno-vation as new 'technologies of power' were devised to govern an embryonic state whose inter-nal (some components sought independence) and external (the very borders of the state were contested) legitimacy was fragile and whose economy was increasingly governed by market relations in the absence of a functioning market system. The August regime was a peculiar hybrid of democratic proceduralism and authoritarian patterns of leadership politics." Richard Sakwa, "The Regime System in Russia," *Contemporary Politics* 3, no. 1 (1997): 13.

24. Yeltsin replaced six prosecutors-general, seven heads of the security service (now the FSB), nine finance ministers, six interior ministers, and three foreign ministers.

25. This period involves half of 1996 and 1997. A reflection of the increase in political influ-ence of the oligarchs was the inclusion of Vladimir Potanin in the government as vice prime minister and the appointment of Boris Berezovsky as executive secretary of the CIS.

26. The myth of the Russian oligarchy was dispelled by the events of August 17, 1998, when during the financial crash the oligarchy essentially ceased to exist as an influential group. Moreover, the oligarchy's dependence on the state and bureaucracy became obvious. One of the biggest oligarchs, Vladimir Potanin, stated directly in this regard: "You know very well that the oligarchs play exactly the role that the authorities in fact want them to fulfil. . . . The authorities are still foremost in relation to any role of business." *Kommersant-Daily,* 9 March 1999.

27. From the very beginning of his rule, Yeltsin governed with the help of favorites, grant-ing them control over the current questions of government and changing them so that he would not become dependent on them. In the role of favorites at various times were Gennady Burbulis, Yury Petrov, Yury Skokov, Anatoly Chubais, Alexander Korzhakov, Oleg Soskovets, and Valentin Yumashev.

28. In his memoir *Midnight Diaries,* Yeltsin acknowledges the decisive role that his daugh-ter played during the last stage of his rule. See Yeltsin, *Prezidentskiy marafon,* p. 43.

29. Between August and September 1998, the Kremlin considered the possibility of invit-ing General Alexander Lebed to assume power. See Shevtsova, *Rezhim Borisa Yel'tsina,* p. 393.

30. Immediately after Primakov was dismissed, 81 percent of those polled did not approve of the dismissal. Only 8 percent did. In a poll about potential candidates for president, Pri-makov had the support of 22 percent of the respondents. Zyuganov was supported by 17 per-cent, Luzhkov by 15 percent, and Yavlinsky by 11 percent. Fond, "Obshchestvennoe mnenie," 23 May 1999, "Itogi," NTV.

31. Yeltsin, *Prezidentskiy marafon,* pp. 422–423.

32. George Breslauer was absolutely right when he wrote: "Yel'tsin was not simply a victim of circumstances; he had *opportunities* to do things differently. He missed them." Breslauer, "Russia at the End of Yel'tsin's presidency," *Post-Soviet Affairs* 16, no. 1 (January-March 2000): 5.

33. In September 1999 after these events, 40 percent of Russian citizens polled ranked the need for "personal security" first among priorities of "social guarantees." Twenty-eight percent did not consider it a priority. "Crime" and "instability" took first place on a list of irritants for Russian citizens, with 47 percent and 46 percent, respectively. VTsIOM poll, *Nezavisimaya gazeta,* 16 December 1999.

34. During the first war in Chechnya between 1994 and 1996 an overwhelming part of society was against the war and for the withdrawal of Russian troops. In January 1995, for example, 54 percent of those polled were in favor of withdrawal, 27 percent supported the introduction of troops, and 19 percent were undecided. Because of that war, 84 percent of those polled were dissatisfied with Yeltsin. See *Interfax,* 26 January 1995. During the second war in Chechnya, 46 percent of those polled supported the introduction of troops into the republic, 43 percent expressed doubts about the purpose of this step, and 11 percent had difficulty answering. VTsIOM polls, 28–31 January 2000. *Polit.ru.*

35. In August 1999, 33 percent of those polled supported Putin's policies; in September it was already 52 percent; and in October 65 percent. At the end of November, 29 percent of those polled supported Putin as a presidential candidate; 17 percent supported Zyuganov; and 13 percent supported Primakov. *Kommersant-Daily,* 16 October 1999.

36. According to a VTsIOM poll, the fact that the president long worked in the KGB-FSB worried only 22 percent of the respondents. Yu. Levada, "Chto schitaem po oseni," *NG-Stsenarii,* 15 November 2000.

37. Putin's relationship while he was still prime minister to the journalist Andrei Babitsky, who was persecuted by the security organs for his professional activities in Chechnya, raises concerns about his commitment to future freedoms. This incident could well be defined as a syndrome of totalitarianism in a pluralistic society.

38. "Zheleznyy Putin," *Kommersant-Daily,* 10 March 2000.

39. In his article laying out his program, published in December 1999, Putin tried to present his positions on Russian problems. He tried to alienate neither the right nor the left. He offered society his version of the statecraft, which combined the old and already long discredited ideas of great-power rule, Russian collectivism, and the amorphous idea of a social contract. It seemed that the new leader was drawn to a formula, which even Yeltsin shunned, of a special path for Russia in the modern world, which in essence has always been part of the ideology of Russian patriots who treated the ideas of Western civilization with suspicion. In his first address in March 2000 to Russian voters, Putin unambiguously accused former Russian leaders, and consequently Yeltsin, of lacking will and of being incapable of creating clear and equal rules of the game for all. This was an obvious attempt to appeal to the protest electorate. In later speeches Putin has tried to avoid unambiguous answers to the most acute and contentious questions, in particular about summing up the results of privatization, about state intervention in the economy, about private ownership of land, and about the political future of Chechnya. He consciously avoided questions that allow him to be identified with a definite political force, and he intently tried to preserve for himself the role of being above the political fray.

40. Michael McFaul, "The Power of Putin," *Current History,* October 2000.

41. Putin won in the first round with 52.94 percent of the vote. His closest rival, Zyuganov, received 29.21 percent of the vote.

42. It is curious that Yeltsin himself and his team, even when Putin began to dismantle their regime, continued to pretend that Putin faithfully continued Yeltsin's affairs, and tried to keep at least partial control over his actions. See Yeltsin, *Prezidentskiy marafon,* pp. 391–396.

43. In October 2000, 44 percent of those polled viewed positively the movement of members of the secret services into high government positions, and 34 percent negatively. Levada, "Chto schitaem po oseni." The very fact is proof of the population's disappointment with the previous makeup of the ruling class.

44. *Ot pervogo litsa. Razgovory s Vladimirom Putinym* (Moscow: Vagrius, 2000), p. 168. (Available in English as Vladimir Putin, *First Person: An Astonishingly Frank Self-Portrait by Russia's President, Vladimir Putin,* trans. Catherine Fitzpatrick [New York: Public Affairs, 2000].)

45. In September 2000, only 11 percent of those polled believed that the authorities were telling the truth about the Kursk, and 79 percent thought the authorities were "hiding the reasons for the tragedy." *NG-Stsenarii,* 15 November 2000.

46. Ibid.

47. VTsIOM polls, 28–31 April 2001. *Polit.ru.*

48. Having limited the field of activity of the opposition or overly independent oligarchs such as Berezovsky and Gusinsky, Putin nevertheless gave friendly oligarchs such as Roman Abramovich and Alexander Mamut the opportunity to continue strengthening their economic positions. According to polls, 54 percent of respondents at the end of 2000 believed that Putin relied on security forces, 25 percent thought he leaned on the Yeltsin "family" for support, and 24 percent said he relied on oligarchs. *NG-Stsenarii,* 15 November 2000.

49. Ibid.

50. Quoted in *Kommersant,* 27 October 2000.

51. Interview with Boris Berezovsky in *Izvestiya,* 3 November 2000.

5

Political Leadership and the Center-Periphery Struggle: Putin's Administrative Reforms

Eugene Huskey

The passing of regimes in the multiethnic expanse of Russia has traditionally produced a crisis in relations between the capital and the
provinces. So it was in the time of troubles at the beginning of the seventeenth century and during the wars and revolutions in the first quarter of the
twentieth century; so it is today in Russia's transition from communism. At
the beginning of the 1990s, most of the ideological, institutional, and
patronage ties that had bound Soviet provincial leaders to central authority
disappeared along with one-party rule. Amid communism's ruins, the leaders of Russia's 89 republics and regions began to claim political, economic,
and cultural autonomy that would have been unthinkable in any modern
state, let alone the old Soviet Union. Inspired by personal ambitions as well
as the localist instincts that had never been far below the surface in the
Soviet era, key provincial elites sought to wrest as much power as they could
from Moscow before the central state was able to establish a new ruling
"vertical."

Facilitating the rise of provincial power in Russia through the 1990s was
the weakness of Yeltsin's leadership and the serious divisions within and
between central executive and legislative institutions. These divisions

encouraged Muscovite elites to outbid each other in the granting of concessions to provincial leaders. The devolution of political power also resulted from three changes in the country's institutional design, changes that strengthened significantly the stature and authority of provincial chief executives. First, Yeltsin's dissolution of the national parliament in the fall of 1993 led to restrictions on legislative power in the republics and regions as well. Emasculating the traditional legislative check on executive leadership encouraged presidents and governors to develop a personalist form of rule, which in turn allowed relatively united provincial political establishments to confront a fissiparous central state.

Second, the constitution of 1993 created an upper chamber, the Federation Council, whose members were the chief executive and assembly speaker in each subject territory. This unusual system of legislative representation enhanced the political capital of the provincial elites by granting them veto power over important presidential appointments, such as the procurator general and constitutional court justices, as well as the ability to block, or at least delay, federal legislation. In effect, the president engineered a constitution that put additional bargaining chips in the hands of provincial politicians. The merging of the role of provincial executive with that of national legislator was an invitation to trade legislative favors for provincial autonomy or privileges. In the slightly exaggerated language of the journalist Irina Kholmskaya, "Yeltsin paid the governors so generously with [transfers of] power that at one point he had nothing left to give."[1]

Until 1996, the ability of the president to hire and fire the country's 68 governors limited the freedom to maneuver of the heads of regional administrations. But the decision to introduce direct gubernatorial elections—a move designed in part to attract the support of provincial elites for Yeltsin's shaky presidential campaign—fundamentally altered Russia's political calculus. In the wake of the gubernatorial elections from 1996 to 1998, governors gained a legitimacy, job security, and political independence that had been lacking in Yeltsin's first term. According to R. F. Turovsky, 1996 produced a "quiet revolution" in center-periphery relations. With a newly acquired democratic legitimacy, "the governor was transformed into a 'mini-president' . . . and [demanded] more economic autonomy and more political power."[2] If one were to identify a single institutional factor that distinguished presidential power in Russia in the late 1990s from the more muscular versions in surrounding post-Soviet states, such as Belarus and Kazakhstan, it would be the direct election of governors. This constraint on presidential patronage power ensured that Russia's political development would differ from that of its more authoritarian neighbors.

By the end of the 1990s, the formal rules of the Russian state, which represented a peculiar mixture of unitary and federal principles, masked relations between center and periphery that were moving in the direction of confederation. Just as the war of laws between all-union and republican legislatures had characterized the end of the Soviet era, so new skirmishes between provincial and federal legislation were breaking out in postcommunist Russia. According to officials in Moscow, fully one-quarter of legal norms emanating from the republics and regions were in violation of federal law.[3] Moreover, provincial authorities were increasingly coopting the federal agencies working in their territories, whether through their ability to vet federal appointees or to provide them with desperately needed goods and services that could not be acquired with their miserly pay packets. By offering access to affordable and decent housing, transportation, and even child care, provincial authorities enjoyed potent levers of influence over federal bureaucrats whose first loyalties should have been to the center. As James Madison observed in Federalist 51 more than two centuries ago, "the members of each department should be as little dependent as possible on those of the others for the emoluments annexed to their offices," lest their independence be "merely nominal."[4] Finally, some presidents and governors insisted on a control of taxes, property, and trade that impeded development of a viable state and national commerce. In the wake of the August 1998 financial crisis, for example, some regions erected protectionist barriers that one normally associates with international economic relations and not intrastate trade.[5]

The Antecedents of Putin's Institutional Reforms

It was against this backdrop of rising provincial power that Vladimir Putin introduced dramatic measures to recentralize political authority immediately after his inauguration as president in May 2000. These initiatives stripped provincial chief executives of their membership in the Federation Council and thereby removed their parliamentary immunity from prosecution; asserted greater central control over local governments operating within the country's republics and regions; and empowered the president to remove provincial chief executives from office if legislation in the territories was not brought into line with federal law or if the chief executives themselves were suspected of a crime. Moreover, on the strength of a single presidential decree, Putin fundamentally reorganized the country's administrative structure by inserting seven federal super-districts between Moscow and the 89 subject territories.

At first glance, these reforms appeared to represent a radical departure from the policies of the Yeltsin era. But Putin's moves were in fact the culmination of a reaction to the decentralization of Russian politics that had begun several years earlier. In a wide-ranging analysis of center-periphery relations near the end of the Yeltsin era, R. F. Turovsky shows that Anatoly Chubais and other young liberal technocrats began a counteroffensive in May–June 1997 against the rise of provincial power. This campaign sought to use two institutions to strengthen the hand of the center: local government and presidential representatives in the regions.[6]

The presence of three layers of government in Russia—federal, provincial, and local—created a triangular game in which the presidency was able to ally itself with local authorities as a means of squeezing or restraining provincial elites. Not only did federal and local authorities have a natural political interest in limiting the powers of provincial leaders, they also supported a policy agenda that was in general more reform-oriented than that championed by republican presidents and regional governors. Where Yeltsin and city mayors shared the same social base of urban voters, presidents and governors were oriented to the more traditional view of the electorate in rural areas and small towns. Recognizing this community of interests between federal and local authorities, the Yeltsin presidency formed a Council of Local Government that sought to organize leading Russian mayors into a partnership with Moscow in the center-periphery struggle.[7] The goal of the partnership, which followed an attempt by Udmurtiya in 1996 to eliminate local governments within their republic, was to open an assault on the presidents and governors from above and below. If provincial elites were intent on preventing federal authorities from establishing a single executive hierarchy that ran from Moscow through the provinces and into the cities and urban districts, then the federal authorities were going to attempt to undo the ruling vertical that presidents and governors were establishing within their own territories. But as Turovsky notes, "scorching the earth under the feet of the provincial elites" encouraged a kind of anarchy in intergovernmental relations. "In their struggle with the political ambitions [of the provincial elites]," he says, "the center was destroying de facto all possibilities for normal administration and subordination."[8]

During the same period, Chubais and other centralizers also sought to counterbalance the rising power of the republican presidents and regional governors by strengthening the representatives of the national president who operated in most of the country's subject territories. Established originally in 1991 to serve as the eyes and ears of the center in provincial affairs, these presidential emissaries had been marginalized as actors in provincial politics by the middle of the 1990s. Operating with a miniscule staff and budget, they found themselves dependent for essential goods and services on the republican presidents and governors whom they were supposed to monitor. Moreover, the first wave of presidential representatives, often democratic activists who arrived in the territories as political outsiders, gave way to a replacement generation that was tied closely to the provincial political establishment.[9]

In an attempt to revive the institution of presidential representative, Yeltsin issued a decree in July 1997 that widened their powers considerably. Henceforth, the presidential representatives, rather than provincial chief executives, were supposed to oversee the disbursement of federal budgetary funds in the territories. Furthermore, the presidential representatives were asked to chair a new collegium in their province that brought together for the first time under one roof the heads of all federal agencies operating within the territory. Depending on the size of the territory, this number ranged from 20 to 54 federal bureau chiefs, who oversaw from 1,500 to 20,000 federal civil servants in each province.[10] There was even a proposal under discussion that would have divided the country into 24 territories for federal monitoring purposes, with a presidential representative to be responsible for several republics or regions at once. Although the radical redesign of Russian political-administrative space would have to await the reforms of the Putin era, the July 1997 decree did anticipate the possibility of a presidential representative assuming responsibilities for several provinces at once, and in the northern Caucasus, a single representative was assigned to monitor five provinces.

The attempt to reclaim authority for the central state through a tactical alliance with local governments and the expansion of the powers of the presidential representatives enjoyed some success in a few provinces. In Ivanovo, for example, the creation of a collegium of federal agency heads did elevate the status of the presidential representative in the region.[11] During the same period, the constitutional court ruled in favor of the centralizers by declaring unconstitutional the Udmurt law that sought to abolish local government institutions. But these measures were unable to reverse the drift toward confederative arrangements, which was rendering the Russian state increasingly ungovernable in the second half of the 1990s.

The failure to sustain the momentum of this centralizing initiative derived from several factors: the deepening infirmity of the president, without whose personal involvement political and administrative elites remained reluctant to pursue reform; the need for the support of provincial elites in the approaching parliamentary and presidential campaigns of 1999 and 2000; and continuing divisions within the central executive, specifically between Viktor Chernomyrdin, the prime minister, and Anatoly Chubais, the presidential chief of staff. As Turovsky explains, in contrast to Chubais's willingness to beat the provincial elites into submission, Chernomyrdin "was oriented toward the establishment of his own client base" among provincial leaders, and was likely to make fewer demands, and when he did so, to use the carrot instead of the stick. The victory of the Chernomyrdin line in federal relations was evident by the end of October 1997, when, in a radio broadcast devoted exclusively to regional affairs, Yeltsin in effect called a halt to the centralizing campaign of Chubais and the young liberal technocrats.[12]

Among this group of centralizers was Vladimir Putin, who, as head of the presidential Monitoring Administration, and later deputy chief of staff in the presidency with special reference to provincial affairs, gained an intimate understanding of the scale of corruption in the provinces and the problems posed by the lack of an efficient executive hierarchy linking Moscow with the rest of the country.[13] On the basis of his experience in the presidential bureaucracy under Yeltsin, Putin in 1998 was

> the first to suggest the idea of the consolidation of regions and the reorganization of the activities of the presidential representatives. . . . Before going on vacation that summer he asked the Territorial Administration to prepare appropriate documents [for such a reform]. But after his vacation, he left for other work, in the FSB [Federal Security Agency], and the project remained unrealized. He would later return to this proposal as president. Thus, the president had thought long about the conceptual underpinnings [*kontseptsiya*] of this reform, and those persons are mistaken who think that this was a poorly thought-out, spontaneous decision. The president adopted it absolutely consciously. Moreover, he knows what still needs to be done, and he understands this more deeply than we can imagine.[14]

Vladimir Putin and the Establishment of a New Ruling Vertical

After the fall of communism, the Russian presidency relied on four major instruments to restrain the autonomy-seeking behavior of provincial elites. These were military force, used most notably in Chechnya; legal norms, including the constitution, federal laws, and constitutional court decisions; bargaining, in which the president traded personal, financial, and political favors to provincial leaders in exchange for their acquiescence to central direction as well as their votes and those of their constituents; and finally a bureaucracy of monitoring and supervision, or in Russian, *kontrol'*, which was essentially an intelligence-gathering operation employing longstanding state institutions, such as the procuracy and the FSB, as well as newly created appendages of the presidency, such as the Monitoring Administration and the presidential representatives. Given Putin's own professional background in the KGB, it is no surprise that in the early weeks of the new administration, he placed unusual emphasis on this last instrument of rule in his relations with the provinces.

Whereas Gorbachev employed glasnost in the mid-1980s as a means of collecting reliable information on political and economic conditions in the country, Putin opted for a new bureaucracy of *kontrol'* that could at once offer the president a more accurate picture of developments in the periphery as well as incriminating evidence (*kompromat*) on provincial leaders. Anchoring this new bureaucracy were presidential representatives with expanded powers and territorial reach, whom we shall refer to as governors-general. Instead of a large corps of politically feeble presidential representatives assigned to the individual republics and regions, Putin appointed a trusted official to the post of governor-general in each of the country's seven new federal superdistricts. One of the first responsibilities of these governors-general was "developing an inventory [*inventarizatsiya*] of the country."[15] Collecting information in the provinces acquired particular importance in light of Putin's legislative initiatives of May 2000, which, as noted earlier, exposed presidents and governors to removal from office if they failed to bring legal norms in their republics and regions in line with federal law or if they were the subject of a criminal investigation. In a country where criminal investigations can easily drag on for months or even years, where criminal prosecution has been a central feature of the political struggle, and where most people are guilty of something anyway—"show me a man and I'll find you an article in the criminal code to match"—the ability to remove an elected official on the strength of suspicion of a crime gave the president a powerful means of neutralizing opposition to his policies. If the governors-general were directly responsible for ensuring that provincial leaders aligned republican and regional legislation with federal laws, they were at least indirectly responsible for exposing provincial elites to prosecution by removing from office local law enforcement officials who had suppressed investigations into wrongdoing by provincial elites.

Putin also appeared determined to reassess, and possibly annul, the bilateral treaties that had been negotiated since 1994 between the federal government and 46 of the subject territories. If the constitution itself had created a system of asymmetrical federalism by granting the country's 21 ethnic republics a higher status than the 68 regions, these follow-on agreements deepened the political and legal inequality among provinces by according certain signatories more cultural, economic, and even military autonomy than others. To quote *Komsomol'skaya pravda* from early September 2000, "sources in the Kremlin do not exclude the possibility that Putin will unilaterally annul 'the most unjust' agreements." Laying the groundwork for such a move, the governor-general for the Northwest Federal District, Viktor Cherkesov, announced that the bilateral treaties "had exhausted themselves politically and, what's more, juridically."[16]

As a gesture of good will to provincial elites who were stunned by the speed and force of the presidential assault on their status and prerogatives, Putin offered two palliatives. Confident that his institutional reforms would impose discipline on the country's presidents and governors, Putin encouraged the provincial executives to establish ruling verticals in their own territories by granting presidents and governors the power to remove miscreant local leaders. But the authority accorded to provincial leaders was not symmetrical with that enjoyed by the Russian president. Not only did the latter possess the ability to dismiss provincial elites who abused their right to remove local-level executives, he could also intervene directly in the affairs of many local governments. According to legislation adopted by the parliament in August 2000, in all cities and districts with more than 50,000 persons, the Russian president could reach over the provincial elites to regulate the "details of the structures of local government."[17] Previously, Moscow had asserted the authority to intervene directly in local government only in areas where national security was at issue, such as border zones or closed cities with secret defense plants.[18]

Second, having rushed through legislation that promised to strip presidents and governors of their national legislative mandate, Putin sought to preserve for them a measure of dignity and visibility by including provincial executives in a newly created State Council.[19] Because the sheer number of provincial executives would make regular State Council meetings unwieldy, the decree on the State Council of September 1, 2000, called for the creation of a presidium to serve as the working core of the State Council. At any time, only a handful of presidents or governors would have seats on the presidium because of its rotating membership. Some observers— including prominent governors like Saratov's Dmitry Ayatskov and even some officials in the presidency—speculated that the State Council would assume some of the powers of the Federation Council, such as vetting presidential nominees or vetoing presidential decrees.[20] Following the first meeting of the presidium of the State Council on September 29, Putin himself volunteered that this consultative body would become a "powerful organ" (*moshchnyy organ*).[21] But given the president's ability to appoint and dismiss members of the presidium every six months, the infrequent meetings of the body (once a month), and the dismal record of earlier incarnations of presidential consultative institutions, it is unlikely that the State Council will offset in any appreciable way the loss of provincial power that has followed from Putin's initiatives.

None of Putin's actions has been more controversial than his May 2000 decree dividing Russia into seven new federal superdistricts, each headed by a governor-general appointed by the president. Designed to reorient the members of Moscow's bureaucracy of *kontrol'* away from provincial power and toward the interests of the president, the measure is fundamentally recasting relations between center and periphery, between government and presidency, and within the presidency itself. It has the potential to become a constitutional revolution by stealth.[22]

As Table 1 illustrates, Russia now has seven mini-governments operating between the federal center and the 89 subject territories. From headquarters in Moscow and six provincial cities, the governors-general monitor political and economic affairs in surrounding provinces. They are ensconced in newly acquired facilities befitting their prominence and stature. Just as American courthouses and federal buildings symbolize the influence of their occupants, so the offices of the new presidential representatives exhibit appropriate physical grandeur. In Khabarovsk, for example, the governor-

Table 1. Russia's Federal Districts

Name	Governor-General	Administrative Center	Constituent Provinces
Central	G. S. Poltavchenko	Moscow	Belgorod, Bryansk, Yaroslavl, Ivanovo, Kaluga, Kostroma, Kursk, Lipetsk, Moscow, Moscow City, Orel, Ryazan, Smolensk, Tambov, Tver', Tula, Vladimir, Voronezh
Far Eastern	K. B. Pulikovsky	Khabarovsk	Amur, Kamchatka, Khabarovsk, Primor'e, Magadan, Sakhalin, Sakha (Yakutiya), Jewish A.O., Koryak A.O., Chukot A.O.
Southern	V. G. Kazantsev	Rostov-na-Donu	Adygeya, Astrakhan, Chechnya, Dagestan, Ingushetiya, Kabardino-Balkariya, Kalmykiya, Karachaevo-Cherkessiya, Krasnodar, Northern Ossetiya (Alaniya), Rostov, Stavropol, Volgograd
Northwest	V. V. Cherkesov	St. Petersburg	Arkhangelsk, Kaliningrad, Kareliya, Komi, Leningrad, Murmansk, Novgorod, Pskov, St.Petersburg City, Vologda, Nenets A.O.
Siberia	L. V. Drachevsky	Novosibirsk	Altay republic, Altay kray, Buryatiya, Chita, Irkutsk, Kemerovo, Khakasiya, Krasnoyarsk, Novosibirsk, Omsk, Tomsk, Tyva, Aginskiy Buryat A.O., Evensk A.O.,Taimir A.O., Ust'-Ordynsk Buryat A.O.
Urals	P. M. Latyshev	Ekaterinburg	Chelyabinsk, Kurgan, Sverdlovsk, Tyumen, Yamalo-Nenets A.O., Khanty-Mansi A.O.
Volga	S. V. Kirienko	Nizhny Novgorod	Bashkortostan, Chuvashiya, Kirov, Marii El, Mordoviya, Nizhegorodskaya, Orenburg, Penzen, Perm, Samara, Saratov, Ul'yanov, Tatarstan, Udmurtiya, Komi-Permyatsk A.O.

general took over a luxury five-story office building in the heart of the city.[23] Not surprisingly, given the shortage of vacant prestige property, housing the governors-general hurriedly in suitable offices provoked controversy. In Ekaterinburg, the governor-general angered many in the local population by expelling from a building a Children's Culture Society, which served 4,000 children, to make way for his entourage.[24]

Although there is a certain economic and political logic to the configuration of the seven super-districts—the Volga terrritory, for example, binds together numerous ethnic republics—the primary reason for the particular territorial divisions lies in Russian military geography. The new federal superdistricts correspond closely to the country's seven military districts, sharing with most of them not just boundaries but headquarters cities. As if this reminder of the ultimate source of federal authority were not sufficient, Putin appointed generals to head five of the seven superdistricts—two from the regular army, two from the security services, and one from the police, or MVD. The two civilian leaders were the young economist, and former prime minister, Sergey Kirienko, who was assigned to Nizhny Novgorod, and Leonid Drachevsky, previously minister for CIS affairs, who was assigned to Novosibirsk.

Trained to carry out orders from above—and unused to the give and take characteristic of democratic politics—the generals "parachuted" into the territories with a fierce determination to carry out the president's mission. The clash between these military traditions and the demands of an open society and competitive politics was evident in their first words and deeds. In his initial interview with the *Obshchaya gazata* correspondent in Khabarovsk, General Konstantin Pulikovsky remarked, "I am available to everyone [*ya otkryt dlya vsekh*]. But bear in mind: people who just once write a falsehood about me no longer exist as far as I'm concerned."[25] During his first visit to the Maritime Province, Pulikovsky dealt harshly with representatives of the provincial government, who had to face the governor-general without their conveniently ill leader, the maverick governor, Yevgeny Nazdratenko. Hearing official protests that the provincial government was forced to subsidize numerous federal institutions, including the Border Guards and the headquarters of the Pacific Fleet, Pulikovsky retorted: "You have no moral right to complain about your burden until the Maritime Province finally becomes self-sufficient and does not require subsidies from the federal budget."[26]

Even before their mission had been fully clarified, the governors-general began to assemble a staff that is scheduled to grow to approximately 100 persons.[27] Among this number are five to seven deputies, who have been drawn from among trusted subordinates and colleagues or well-connected officials from the territories themselves.[28] Where Kirienko hired economists and lawyers, the generals pressed into service their uniformed colleagues. Thus, in the Northwest Federal District, General Cherkesov selected his deputies from among former colleagues in the FSB.[29] The differences in style between the governors-general were evident in the method of recruiting staff, with the young Kirienko employing the Internet to attract a flood of applications.[30] In contrast, among the 500 applications submitted for vacancies in the governor-general's office in Khabarovsk were pleas like the following: "I have just been demobilized and would like to work under the command of General Pulikovsky."[31]

In the headquarters of the governors-general worked subordinate personnel who had responsibility for support services, specific policy issues, or a particular geographical area—the latter akin to zonal inspectors in the old Communist Party apparatus. Again as in the old regime, staff were assigned to answering letters from the populace—600 of which arrived each month in the office of the governor-general of the Far East Federal District alone. In contrast to the communist practice, however, the office did not forward (*otfutbolirovat'*) those letters to lower-level officials about whom the complaints were lodged.[32]

Other staff members worked full-time in the individual subject territories. In the Central Federal District, fourteen of the territory's eighteen republics or regions had "chief federal inspectors" in place by the beginning of September; the number was four of ten in the Far East District.[33] Such inspectors were assigned to a single province if the territory was unusually large or ethnically diverse, but in most cases a chief federal inspector assumed responsibility for several republics or regions. Thus, in the Southern Federal District, one chief federal inspector covered three provinces: Volgograd, Astrakhan, and Kalmykiya. It appears that subordinate federal inspectors were working in each subject territory. The new system of *kontrol'* retained, therefore, monitors on the ground, though these individuals, many of whom were the incumbent presidential representatives, no longer reported directly to the Kremlin but to its seven territorial branches. Besides the old presidential representatives, the offices of the governors-general also brought under their wing presidential officials from the Monitoring Administration and the Cadres Administration who were based in the provinces.[34] Transferring these personnel to the new bureaucracies in the seven federal districts threatened to diminish the influence of presidential bureaus on Old Square in Moscow by cutting direct ties with their officers in the field.

In one sense, the governors-general operated as a link in the presidential bureaucracy between agents on the ground and officials in Moscow. But such a description fails to capture the full measure of their responsibilities or stature. The governors-general were not just managers in a bureaucracy of *kontrol'* but federal diplomats in charge of personal liaison with republican presidents and regional governors.[35] As the governor-general of the Central Federal District, Georgy Poltavchenko, observed: "One of my main tasks is to work with governors individually as well as collectively."[36] And the governors-general were in most respects politically equal, if not superior, to the elected presidents and governors within their territories.[37] Shortly after arriving at their new headquarters, each governor-general began scheduling get-acquainted visits to surrounding presidents and governors, with speculation mounting that in the future it would be the provincial executives who would be seeking out the governors-general.[38]

Besides carrying out "diplomatic" and *kontrol'* functions, the governors-general serve as the leaders of newly opened collegia of government ministries and agencies in the seven federal territories. No sooner had Putin decreed the creation of the new territories than Moscow ministries began announcing the establishment of subdivisions in St. Petersburg, Moscow, Nizhny Novgorod, Rostov, Ekaterinburg, Novosibirsk, and Khabarovsk. The first branches to open were those associated with legal institutions, such as the procuracy and the ministry of justice, and the power ministries, such as the ministry of defense, internal affairs, the tax police, and the FSB. The latter had always been subordinate in operational terms to the president rather than the prime minister. But by the end of the summer of 2000, many other ministries had jumped on the bandwagon. In the Southern Federal District, General Viktor Kazantsev created a collegium of 24 persons, which included his deputies, the head of the Northern Caucasus Military District, and the leaders of federal district and provincial departments of power ministries such as the MVD, FSB, FPS, and customs service.[39] The seven cities were emerging as mini-Moscows, with the governors-general aspiring to play the role of territorial chief executives.

By creating a new, dense layer of federal bureaucracy in the seven territories, the center sought to reclaim the loyalties of the army of federal civil servants who worked in the provinces. Although the center had attempted to achieve this goal at the end of the 1990s, in part by directing presidential representatives to chair collegia of federal officials in each republic or region, federal personnel outside of Moscow had remained under the influence of provincial chief executives, who vetted the appointment of federal officials and ensured their well-being, including providing gratis such basic goods as utilities for their buildings.[40] In bringing Moscow closer to the provinces by establishing these seven federal outposts, the reform was designed to diminish the isolation and vulnerability felt by the agents of federal power, serving in what were often personalist or authoritarian regimes in the provinces.

Vladimir Putin and the Law of Unintended Consequences

If the intent of Putin's institutional reform is clear, the effect on the political system remains uncertain a year into the new order. The president's initiatives have clearly reduced considerably the role of provincial elites as actors in national politics. In the face of young, vigorous, and determined leadership from the center, most presidents and governors capitulated with surprising speed.[41] But vital questions remain to be answered about the tenor of relations between the levels of government and the future role for provincial leaders in Russian politics. Will the State Council develop into a vehicle of influence for provincial chief executives? Will the outposts of federal power in the seven districts become more muscular and independent? And will the courts, and especially the constitutional court, serve as agents of a federal consolidation? Actions of the constitutional court in the weeks following the Putin initiatives suggest that justices are prepared to cooperate in the reassertion of federal authority. In a decision from early June 2000, the constitutional court ruled that the Altay republic's claims of sovereignty relating to property and other issues were unfounded.[42] In a special ruling that followed this decision, the justices held that certain provisions of the constitutions of six republics relating to sovereignty were also in violation of federal constitutional principles.[43]

Another vital issue yet to be resolved is the extent to which governors-general will involve themselves in the management of the economy. Thus far, the seven presidential representatives are sending contradictory signals about their interest in economic affairs. If General Pulikovsky in Khabarovsk seems content merely to oversee the expenditure of federal budget funds in his territory, Petr Latyshev in Ekaterinburg believes he has a broader mandate. In his words, "No matter how much we talk today about strengthening vertical relations in the state, in the final analysis one must be focused on raising the efficiency of the economy."[44] In addition to vetting the expenditure of federal funds and overseeing—in some federal districts—the distribution of winter supplies to the Far North, the offices of the governors-general will also play a role in coordinating federal economic management in their territories by virtue of their leadership of the collegia of federal officials. Some will also be tempted, no doubt, to intervene in matters of state property, whether in its sale or the management of enterprises where the state holds a controlling stake.[45] Indeed, according to a source in the Russian White House, the offices of the governors-general "are prepared to assume full responsibility for supervising those bodies that deal with property disputes and the bankruptcy procedures of enterprises."[46]

Political recruitment of provincial officials, whether through election or personnel appointments, is also a prime concern of the governors-general. According to General Pulikovsky, his task during elections is to ensure "equal conditions for candidates for any [elected] position," which means, in his view, preventing incumbents from using "their administrative clout [*administrativnaya vlast'*] and their ability to appear more frequently on television screens."[47] If fully implemented, such a policy would grant the center enormous influence in electoral contests across the country and would in fact assist the challengers promoted by Moscow. However, the results of recent gubernatorial elections reveal that many incumbents disliked by the Kremlin retained their posts. According to Larisa Aydinova, "the recently completed elections, for all their diversity, produced only one surprise: the Kremlin was not able to achieve the task it had set for itself. In a whole number of regions, persons with whom the Kremlin was 'uncomfortable' came to power or remained in power."[48] Of the 44 provincial chief executives whose seats were contested in the 2000 gubernatorial races, all but fifteen won re-election.[49] According to Robert Orttung, "perhaps the most obvious failure of Putin's first-year federal policies was the federal government's inability to shape the outcome of . . . the gubernatorial elections."[50]

Although Putin claimed that the Kremlin "has not had, does not have, and cannot have a special relationship with a gubernatorial candidate," his own behavior during the gubernatorial elections of 2000—as well as that of his subordinates—illustrated that the presidency was by no means a mere observer of electoral politics in the provinces.[51] For example, during a visit to Kaliningrad, Putin made it clear that he preferred Admiral Yegorov to the incumbent governor—and candidate for re-election—Leonid Gorbenko.[52] In the Perm region, where a young and energetic mayor sympathetic to Putin captured the governorship, the governor-general repeatedly commented during the campaign that the federal authorities could work well with such a candidate.[53] And in the Tyumen region, the first deputy governor-general stood for the governorship, clearly with the support of his boss and the Kremlin. The president's claims to electoral neutrality may fit nicely with the mythology of a Gaullist-style leader who stands above the political fray, but it conflicts with Russian reality and, indeed, with electoral politics in most democratic societies.

It remains unclear what role, if any, presidential officials played in the disqualification of candidates like Alexander Rutskoy, the former governor of the Kursk region and a leader of the opposition to Yeltsin. On the eve of the election in Kursk, the regional court disqualified Rutskoy for making false statements on his property disclosure form—denying the ownership of two automobiles and understating the value of a Moscow apartment. With Rutskoy out of the running, the race was won by Alexander Mikhaylov, who proceeded to embarrass the Kremlin by uttering anti-Semitic statements while pledging his support for Putin, another "ethnic Russian" like himself. Whether or not the Kremlin had a hand in the anti-Rutskoy campaign, presidential officials were quick to condemn the new governor's behavior. Within days, Mikhaylov had been called on the carpet by the governor-general, Poltavchenko, who criticized Mikhaylov's "scandalous statements to the press."[54]

The involvement of the governors-general in appointive, as opposed to electoral, politics appears to be an even higher priority for Putin. By Yeltsin's second term in office, provincial chief executives had acquired the power to veto the regional appointments of federal ministries, much as the party first secretaries had done in the Soviet era. In some cases, the presidents and governors were able to convince central agencies to select their preferred candidates, especially for critical law enforcement posts such as the procurator. Together with their growing influence over the local media, the ability of presidents and governors to keep independent-minded legal officials out of their territories facilitated the rise of personalist regimes. In Putin's words, this encroachment of provincial officials on federal personnel decisions "led to an obvious shift [of loyalties] from the federal center and to the erosion of a common economic and legal space . . . [which] was one of the country's main problems."[55]

In order to eliminate entrenched networks of corruption and protectionism, Putin believed that it was essential to reorient provincially based federal officials toward Moscow. To achieve this end, the governors-general have begun to insist that they, rather than the presidents and governors, should vet the provincial appointees of federal ministries. In some cases, they have engineered the removal of key provincial officials, like the procurator, without consulting the affected president or governor.[56] Not surprisingly, these incursions into the all-important field of patronage policy have prompted a vigorous reaction from many provincial leaders, including the president of Bashkortostan, Murtaz Rakhimov, and the governor of the Sverdlovsk region, Eduard Rossel. At a meeting in October 2000, Rossel condemned the "muscle flexing" of the governor-general, Latyshev, who had arranged the removal of federal officers in Sverdlovsk without consulting Rossel. Rossel complained that Latyshev had replaced experienced personnel with individuals "who hadn't managed three chickens in their lives."[57]

Perhaps the most extraordinary example of federal interference in elite recruitment in the provinces was the removal of Yevgeny Nazdratenko as governor of the Maritime Province in early February 2001. The poster boy for provincial resistance to federal power, Nazdratenko had presided over the economic meltdown of his region and, as a result, had been the subject of fierce criticism from Moscow for years. Although Putin could have removed Nazdratenko from office by subjecting him to criminal prosecution—there was apparently plenty of *kompromat*—or by claiming that the territory's legislation was not in accord with federal law, he chose instead to employ a more humane method associated with the circulation of members of the Soviet *nomenklatura*: he found him a new job, as head of the State Committee on Fisheries in Moscow. Thus, through bribe and blackmail rather than forcible dismissal, the president removed the longstanding nemesis of federal power in the Russian Far East.

To ensure that Nazdratenko's lieutenants did not continue the policies of their patron, the office of Pulikovsky, the governor-general, launched an immediate assault on Nazdratenko's political allies in the region. Following a "tough [*zhestkiy*] conversation" with Pulikovsky, six deputy governors allied to Nazdratenko resigned. The next targets of the governor-general were the other pillars of Nazdratenko's personalist regime—the leaders of local law enforcement agencies and the press. According to the *Kommersant-Daily* correspondent in Vladivostok, by mid-February Pulikovsky was "de facto in full charge of [*polnost'yu kontroliruet*] executive authority in the Maritime Province."[58]

Given Putin's intense focus on recasting relations between Moscow and the provinces, it is noteworthy that his institutional reforms have done little to clarify the lines of authority for provincial affairs within the presidency itself.[59] To put the issue more precisely, Putin has attended to the provincial oversight apparatus of the presidency in Moscow while seeming to ignore the problem of jurisdictional conflicts between that apparatus and the new governors-general in the seven federal districts. One of Putin's first actions as president was to simplify the presidential bureaucracy in Moscow as it relates to the subject territories. Introducing a reform that he had first suggested two years earlier, while serving in the Executive Office of the President,[60] Putin merged three presidential institutions—the Territorial Administration, the Administration for Coordinating the Activity of Presidential Representatives, and the Administration for Local Government Issues—into a single Main Territorial Administration. At the beginning of 2001, the head of the Main Territorial Administration, Yevgeny Samoylov, answered up the chain of command to Alexander Abramov, at deputy chief of staff, who in turn reported to Alexander Voloshin, the president's chief of staff, known formally as the Leader of the Executive Office of the President (*rukovoditel' Administratsii Prezidenta*).[61]

Although the Main Territorial Administration included the old Administration for Coordinating the Activity of Presidential Representatives, the raison d'etre for the latter body disappeared with the elimination of the provincial-based presidential representatives. Whereas under Yeltsin the provincial-level presidential representatives reported to the Administration for Coordinating the Activity of Presidential Representatives, the offices of the new governors-general became "independent subdivisions of the Executive Office of the Presidency."[62] In the second half of 2000, the Main Territorial Administration did attempt to establish some measure of direct oversight of the governors-general by forming seven new departments, one for each of the federal superdistricts, but the governors-general refused to submit themselves or their offices to the scrutiny of the Main Territorial Administration. The only bureau of the Executive Office that appears to have direct relations with the offices of the governors-general is the Administration of Affairs, which procures office space and transportation in the seven federal districts.[63] The involvement of the Main Territorial Administration in the new institutional reforms seems to be restricted thus far to assisting in the formation of the State Council.[64]

Salaries and civil service rankings reveal the standing of the offices of the governors-general in the larger presidential bureaucracy. Where the governors-general themselves are equal in rank to a first deputy leader of the Executive Office of the President, the first deputies of the governors-general are on the level of a deputy chief of the presidential staff, whose numbers include the head of the influential Main State-Legal Administration. In an apparent attempt to attract the best talent to the new federal district bureaucracies, Putin has introduced a pay scale that is substantially higher than that enjoyed by Moscow-based presidential officials. The pay of a chief federal inspector, whose rank is deputy governor-general, equals that of a deputy chief of the presidential staff in Moscow, who is a full rung higher on the civil service ladder. Where the chief federal inspector receives 3000 rubles in base pay, his counterpart in rank in Moscow receives only 1700–1800.[65] For their part, the governors-general receive a base salary of 9450 rubles a month, making them among the best paid officials in the country.[66]

In seeking to establish a more effective bureaucracy of presidential *kontrol'*, Putin unwittingly created institutions that have emerged as competitors rather than subordinates or partners to the presidential bureaucracy in Moscow. While remaining loyal to Putin the president, the governors-general have little interest in submitting themselves to the authority of the apparatus of the presidency.[67] According to Marina Kalashnikova, the speed with which the governors-general set about establishing their offices reflected in part their "desire to avoid a scheme of management of the federal districts that is now being hurriedly composed in the presidential apparatus [in Moscow]."[68] The tension between the strong-willed governors-general and the bureaucrats in the Kremlin and Old Square was evident in the reaction of officials in the Main State-Legal Administration to General Pulikovsky's formation of a Council of the Federal District in the Far East, whose members included the provincial chief executives in the territory. To Pulikovsky's claim that Putin himself had approved the creation of such a body, a source in the Main State-Legal Administration responded that "the words of Pulikovsky are clearly in need of a legal foundation [*otlivka*]. In principle, granting any council executive functions is not allowed under current legislation."[69] Internal conflicts in the presidency also revealed themselves during the gubernatorial elections, when in some regions a governor-general supported one candidate while the Kremlin apparatus in Moscow backed another.[70] In constructing a new vertical, Putin still had work to do within the presidency itself.[71]

Putin took a small step in the direction of clarifying lines of authority within the presidency at the end of January 2001, when he issued a decree that strengthened the hand of the presidential chief of staff vis-à-vis the governors-general. The decree granted the chief of staff explicit authority to decide questions concerning "relations between the presidential representatives and their own bureaucracies as well as between [the representatives] and other subdivisions of the presidential apparatus." To emphasize this point, the decree subjected the governors-general not only to the "Constitution, federal statutes, and the decrees and directives of the President," but also to the "directives and other decisions of the Leader of the Executive Office of the President."[72] But while the Kremlin was consolidating its political control of the governors-general, it was planning to limit its ability to monitor them administratively. By all accounts, in February 2001, Putin was preparing to reduce dramatically the size of the Main Territorial Administration and transfer some of its personnel to the offices of the governors-general.[73]

In formal administrative terms, the lines of communication and authority ran directly from the governors-general to the chief of staff in the wake of the January decree. But complicating this neat chain of command in the first year of the Putin presidency was an informal political axis that linked the governors-general to the head of the Security Council, Sergey Ivanov. Unlike Voloshin, Ivanov was a Putin loyalist with a professional background and interests that overlapped those of several of the governors-general, who regarded Ivanov as their "informal boss."[74] With the appointment of Ivanov as defense minister in March 2001, it appeared likely that Putin would revert to the management of the governors-general through the more formal conduit of the Executive Office of the President.

Beyond the presidency itself, considerable uncertainty surrounds relations between the new governors-general and the prime minister and his government bureaucracy in Moscow. Not only have the governors-general become something akin to prime ministers in their territories, coordinating the work of the newly opened branches of central ministries, they also attend meetings with the Russian government at least once a month.[75] Following the same institutional logic, the seven federal district representatives of some central institutions, such as the procuracy, sit on these agencies' collegia in Moscow with the rank of deputy ministers.

The prominence of these territorial officers in the life of the Russian government threatens to shift power out of Moscow and toward the periphery. It also promises to elevate presidential institutions, whose staff are not constitutional officers, even further above the government and its ministries, whose organizations and officials are subject to parliamentary review. Attempts by the government to assign its own emissaries to the seven federal districts failed because of a vigorous reaction from the presidential apparatus in Moscow, which argued that such a move would create a system of "dual power" in the territories.[76] The absence of government intermediaries in the seven federal districts means, of course, that lower-level agencies of the government and its ministries will be subject to an awkward dual subordination, with the governors-general competing with the prime minister and his staff for the attention of the federal civil service. In the view of one observer, an August 2000 directive from the prime minister on cooperation with the governors-general marked "the removal of real power from the government and its chairman." Among other things, the directive "obliges [the government] to receive the approval of the governors-general for officials appointed in the [federal] districts." And "in all ministries and agencies special departments will be created for coordinating work with the presidential emissaries."[77]

As Nikolay Poroskov observed, Putin's creation of seven federal districts "sets in motion virtually all structures of state,"[78] and where they will come to rest in the new institutional order is not clear. For all of the upheavals in Russia's economy, politics, and national identity in the last twelve years, the administrative framework of the country had remained intact until May 2000. Putin's reliance on political-administrative reform as a means of regathering power in the center reveals the depth of Russia's crisis and the inadequacy of existing institutions to deal with it, just as Nikita Khrushchev's experiment with the *sovnarkhoz* reform did in the late 1950s. Whether the new Russian prefects will facilitate or impede the rise of a modern and democratic state in Russia remains an open question. What is certain is that Putin's administrative reforms have produced unintended—and potentially dysfunctional—consequences in the internal politics of the presidency and in the presidency's already awkward ties to the government. In an attempt to harmonize relations between levels of government, the formation of seven mini-Moscows has disturbed the fragile equilibrium within the Russian executive itself. It has also introduced a wild card in the intricate political game between center and periphery. Among the many outcomes of this new game, as Mikhail Afanasyev warns, is that "the presidential representatives will develop into the chief lobbyists for the interests of the provincial leaders who are subordinated to them."[79] It would be the ultimate irony if Putin's political-administrative reform, designed to regather the Russian lands, created new and potent loyalties, identities, and autonomy-seeking centers of political authority outside of Moscow.

This chapter grew out of a study commissioned by Peter Reddaway and Robert Orttung for their project "State-Building in Russia: The Regional Dimension," which was supported by the Russia Initiative of the Carnegie Corporation. My thanks to Joel Moses for insights and materials on Russia's gubernatorial elections and to Archie Brown, Peter Reddaway, and Bob Sharlet for perceptive comments on an earlier draft of this chapter.

Notes

1. Irina Kholmskaya, "Konets federal'noy razdroblennosti," *Vlast'*, 1 August 2000, p. 16.

2. R. F. Turovskiy, "Otnosheniya 'Tsentr-Regiony' v 1997-1998gg.: mezhdu konfliktom i konsensusom," *Politiya* (Spring 1998): 1, 3.

3. Some put the number even higher. At the end of 1997, Sergey Stepashin, then head of the MVD, claimed that a third of the 9,000 provincial laws examined by his office violated the Russian constitution or federal law. Cited in Cameron Ross, "Federalizm i demokratizatsiya v Rossii," *Polis*, no. 3 (1999): 22. Ross's article offers an excellent analysis of the problems of federalism in transition regimes.

4. *The Federalist Papers* (New York: New American Library, 1961), p. 321.

5. Kathryn Stoner-Weiss noted that "the imposition of price controls, trade restrictions, and threats of tax withholding in many regions since August 17, 1998 have made some analysts and observers harken back to the Russia of the early 1990s, when the survival of the Russian state appeared to be at serious risk." "Central Weakness and Provincial Autonomy: Observations on the Devolution Process in Russia," *Post-Soviet Affairs*, no. 1 (1999): 87.

6. Turovskiy, "Otnosheniya 'Tsentr-Regiony' v 1997-1998gg," 4–8, 15–20.

7. See Eugene Huskey, *Presidential Power in Russia* (Armonk, N.Y.: M. E. Sharpe, 1999), pp. 189–190. For an excellent analysis of the provincial elite's position between federal and local power, see Jean-Charles Lallemand, "Politics for the Few: Elites in Bryansk and Smolensk," *Post-Soviet Affairs,* no. 4 (1999): 312–335.

8. Turovskiy, "Otnosheniya 'Tsentr-Regiony' v 1997-1998gg," 9.

9. Huskey, *Presidential Power in Russia,* pp. 192–193.

10. The federal civil servants represent from 8 to 12 percent of the total number of provincial bureaucrats in each territory.

11. Personal interview with Yuriy Mikhaylovich Voronov, Deputy Governor of Ivanovo Oblast, 7 August 2000, Ivanovo.

12. Turovskiy, "Otnosheniya 'Tsentr-Regiony' v 1997-1998gg," 7, 17.

13. On Putin's rise to power and his launching of reforms to diminish the power of the provinces, parliament, and oligarchs, see Eugene Huskey, "Overcoming the Yeltsin Legacy: Vladimir Putin and Russian Political Reform," chapter 6 of *Contemporary Russian Politics: A Reader,* ed. Archie Brown (Oxford and New York: Oxford University Press, 2001), 82–96.

14. Marina Kalashnikova, "Sergey Samoylov: Gossovet budet rabotat' v Kremle," *Nezavisimaya gazeta,* 2 August 2000, p. 1.

15. Tat'yana Vitebskaya and Yelena Maydanova, "Kirienko i komissiya po bor'be s kleshchem," *Vek,* no. 31 (2000): 3.

16. Aleksandr Gamov, "Koridory vlasti. Prezident ne zhaluet lyubimchikov Yel'tsina," *Komsomol'skaya pravda,* 7 September 2000, p. 2. Apparently, several bilateral treaties are due to expire in the next year and a half.

17. Zakonoproekt, "O vnesenii izmeneniy i dopolneniy v Federal'nyy zakon 'Ob obshchikh printsipakh organizatsii mestnogo samoupravleniya v Rossiyskoy Federatsii'," *Gazeta.ru,* 9 June 2000. See also the "poyasnitel'naya zapiska k proektu" in the same issue of *Gazeta.ru.*

18. For a critique of the proposed law, see Vsevolod Vasil'ev, "Mestnoe samoupravlenie i federal'naya vlast'," *Nezavisimaya gazeta,* 14 June 2000. For an attempt by Putin's allies to undermine the authority of the president's nemesis, the elected mayor of St. Petersburg, Vladimir Yakovlev, by establishing a new post of chair of city government, see Vadim Nesvizhskiy, "Gubernatora Yakovleva lishat vlasti," *Segodnya* Online, 19 May 2000, and Aleksey Makarin, "Strashnaya mest'," *Segodnya,* 31 May 2000.

19. O Gosudarstvennom sovete Rossiyskoy Federatsii, *Sobranie zakonodatel'stva,* no. 36 (2000), st. 3633. Some governors were also worried about the effects of the changes on policy as well as power. As Saratov's governor, Dmitriy Ayatskov, observed, the Federation Council had played "a stabilizing role, exerting restraint on the radicals in the presidential entourage as well as the leftist majority in the State Duma." Dmitriy Ayatskov, Vladimir Dines, and Aleksandr Nikolaev, "Rossiyskiy federalizm: vzglyad iz regiona," *Vlast',* no. 1 (1999): 6.

20. Konstantin Katanyan, "Politika/ekonomika. Ayatskov predlozhil 'optimal'nuyu model gosudarstvennogo ustroystva," *Vremya MN,* 7 September 2000, p. 3. For similarly overly sanguine comments on this body from Moscow Mayor Yuriy Luzhkov and Bashkortostan President Murtaz Rakhimov, see Svetlana Ofitova, "Kollektivnyy konsul'tant Kremlya. Vladimir Putin nadelil regional'nykh liderov novymi polnomochiyami," *Segodnya,* 2 September 2000, p. 1.

21. Vitaliy Tseplyaev, "Politika: novye vyzovy Kremlyu," *Argumenty i fakty,* 4 October 2000.

22. Lilia Shevtsova calls Putin's measures a "coup from within the regime" [*vnutrirezhimniy perevorot*]. "Vsesil'noe bessil'noe prezidentstvo. Za ogranichenie svobod i vol'nostey vlast' dolzhna platit'," *Segodnya,* 9 August 2000, p. 4. Putin seems willing to entertain the idea of constitutional revisions, but only after the pieces of the new institutional order are already in place. Thus, he is prepared to change Russia's model of government through laws and decrees and then update the constitution to reflect those changes. Nikolay Fedorov, the president of Chuvashiya and former minister of justice, attacked Putin for stating that the "Constitution is not a sacred cow." "Politicheskie sdelki sil'nee Konstitutsii," *Segodnya,* 3 August 2000, p. 4.

23. Lyudmila Baklagina, "Oni v koridorakh. Ot kremlya i do Amura my prolozhim vertikal'," *Obshchaya gazeta,* 7 September 2000, p. 7. Each governor-general's office will have at least 3000

square meters, slightly under the 5000 square meters given over to the provincial administration in Khabarovsk. Security will be provided by the Federal Security Service, which guards the Kremlin in Moscow. Petr Akopov, "Namestnikov poshlyut na otselenie," *Izvestiya*, 26 May 2000, p. 3.

24. Sergey Shevaldin, "Reforme gosvlasti meshaet kvartirnyy vopros," *Segodnya*, 29 July 2000, p. 2. In Nizhny Novgorod, Sergey Kirienko established his headquarters in one wing of the former oblast Komsomol offices. According to one report, the local governor, Ivan Sklyarov, is building for Kirienko a new personal residence on the outskirts of the city in the fashionable "Green City" park district. Yelena Tokareva, "Polet namestnika poverkh bar'erov," *Obshchaya gazeta*, 10–16 August 2000, pp. 1, 7.

25. Baklagina, "Oni v koridorakh," p. 7.

26. Oleg Zhunusov, "Polpred provel 'razvedku boem'. Konstantin Pulikovskiy vpervye posetil Primorskiy kray s rabochim vizitom," *Izvestiya*, 10 October 2000, p. 3.

27. "Aleksandr Abramov: Gubernatorov ne budut gonyat' kak zaytsev," *Izvestiya*, 26 May 2000, pp. 1, 3. The decree setting out the structure and functions of the office of the governors-general is *O polnomochnom predstavitele Prezidenta Rossiyskoy Federatsii v federal'nom okruge, Sobranie zakonodatel'stva*, no. 20 (2000), st. 2112.

28. In the Northwest Federal District, the governor-general, V. V. Cherkesov, appointed two first deputies and five deputies. "Vperedi 'sto dney' polpreda prezidenta," *St-Peterburgskie vedomosti*, 4 August 2000, p. 2.

29. Vadim Nesvizhskiy, "Apparat polpreda—filial FSB. Predstavitel' prezidenta v Severo-Zapadnom okruge prizval v zamy soratnikov," *Segodnya*, 1 August 2000, p. 2.

30. More than 3000 persons submitted applications for jobs with Kirienko's office in response to the Internet listing and advertisements in the press. This number was winnowed to 88 by psychologists and others in the office of the governor-general. Among those appointed by Kirienko were Nikolay Mart'yanov, the former acting presidential representative in the Kirov region, who became the chief federal inspector for that region, and Aleksey Meshcheryakov, who became a federal inspector in the Nizhegorodskiy region, having worked previously as the chief counsel of the Samara zhirkombinat. Mariya Samovarova, "Kirienko nabral rezervistov," *Kommersant-Daily*, 28 July 2000, p. 2.

31. Baklagina, "Oni v koridorakh," p. 7.

32. Tamara Shkel', "Ot Moskvy do samykh do okrain. Konstantin Pulikovskiy: ya polpred dal'nevostochnyy, vashenskiy," *Rossiyskaya gazeta*, 9 September 2000, p. 3. By the end of the summer of 2000, the offices of the governors-general were already reporting the results of their investigations into the extent to which provincial legislation conflicted with federal law. Based on material compiled by the Procuracy and Ministry of Justice, officials in the Volga Federal District reported that 567 legislative acts of provinces within their purview did not correspond to the federal constitution or federal law. "Ot Moskvy do samykh do okrain. Vesti iz okrugov," *Rossiiskaya gazeta*, 9 September 2000, p. 3.

33. "Ot Moskvy do samykh do okrain. Vesti iz okrugov," p. 3; and Shkel', "Ot Moskvy do samykh do okrain. Konstantin Pulikovskiy," p. 3.

34. Kalashnikova, "Sergey Samoylov"; and *O polnomochnom predstavitele Prezidenta Rossiyskoy Federatsii v federal'nom okruge.*

35. The governors-general were called many things: *namestniki*, which conjured up the emissaries of the tsar; *polpredy*, which harkened back to the early Bolshevik plenipotentiary representatives of the center; and even "provincial ambassadors" (*regional'nye posly*).

36. Svetlana Sukhova, "Zhestkikh raznoglasiy net. No dlya vozdeystviya na gubernatorov est' konkretnye rychagi," *Segodnya,* 21 July 2000, p. 2.

37. In a recent poll of Russia's elite, all but one governor-general was placed near the middle of the country's 100 most influential politicians—ahead of all but the most prominent republican presidents and regional governors. The exception was Leonid Drachevskiy, who tied for 86th place with Moscow regional governor, Boris Gromov. "100 vedushchikh politikov Rossii v dekabre," *Nezavisimaya gazeta,* 30 December 2000, p. 8. Unlike the presidents and governors, the governors-general enjoyed standing membership on the new State Council.

38. One of Putin's first assignments to the governors-general was to gauge the desires of the provincial executives regarding the membership and functions of the new State Council. Kalashnikova, "Sergey Samoylov."

39. "Kazantsev sozdal novyy organ—kollegiyu," *Novye izvestiya,* 30 August 2000, p. 2. At the same time, Kazantsev created a consultative organ in the Southern Federal District that bears some resemblance to the State Council at the federal level. The Council of Elders will draw members from each of the thirteen provinces in the Southern Federal District and they will be subject to rotation every six months. Andrey Rakul' and Irina Khansivarova, "Novosti: Polpred Kazantsev obrastaet organami," *Kommersant-Daily,* 30 August 2000, p. 2. A similar organ was created in the Siberian Federal District by the governor-general, Leonid Drachevskiy, though here the members included the heads of all provincial executives and legislatures. It is not yet clear how divergent the structures and operations of the seven bureaucracies will be, though "from the comments of the governors-general and their entourage . . . the Center is not limiting them to a single structure and is allowing them to act as circumstances dictate." Marina Kalashnikova, "U polpredov poyavilis' svoi sovety. Novym strukturam otdadut nekotorye funktsii ispolnitel'noy vlasti," *Nezavisimaya gazeta,* 4 August 2000, p. 3.

40. "Perestroyka: v kraynem sluchae prezident rassudit," *Kommersant-Vlast',* 15 August 2000, p. 14.

41. One reason for the deference shown to the Putin initiatives may be the desire of incumbent provincial chief executives not to compromise their chances for re-election. As some observers note, should the incumbents win in the upcoming elections, they may be more willing to resist the assault of the center on their prerogatives. See Avtandil Tsuladze, "Kolpak dlya regionov," *Segodnya,* 11 May 2000, and Indira Dunaeva, "Sem' raz otmer' i rezh'," *NovayaGazeta.ru,* 18 May 2000.

42. Po delu o proverke konstitutsionnosti otdel'nykh polozheniy Konstitutsii Respubliki Altay i Federal'nogo zakona 'Ob obshchikh printsipakh organizatsii zakonodatel'nykh (predstavitel'nykh) i ispolnitel'nykh organov gosudarstvennoy vlasti sub'ektov Rossiiskoy Federatsii, *Sobranie zakonodatel'stva,* no. 25 (2000), st. 2728.

43. Po zaprosu gruppy deputatov Gosudarstvennoy Dumy o proverke sootvetstviya Konstitutsii RF otdel'nykh polozheniy konstitutsii Respubliki Adygeya, Respubliki Bashkortostan, Respubliki Ingushetiya, Respubliki Komi, Respubliki Severnaya Osetiya-Alaniya i Respubliki Tatarstan, *Sobranie zakonodatel'stva,* no. 29 (2000), st. 3117. See also Yelena Mikhaylova and Vladimir Nikolaev, "Regional'nye vozhdi opravlyayutsia," *Segodnya,* 5 August 2000, p. 3. The chairman of the Supreme Court, Vyacheslav Lebedev, has plans to create a new system of administrative courts in the seven federal districts. They would not exist at lower administrative levels. Svetlana Sukhova, "Reforma gosvlasti vynesena na administrativnyy sud. Dela protiv

gubernatorov budut rassmatrivat'sya v spetsial'nykh sudakh," *Segodnya,* 2 August 2000, p. 2. In the words of Lebedev, the reform has already received the approval of the president. Ibid.

44. Aleksandr Chechevishnikov, "Polpred ili 'polupred'? Luchshe ispravlyat' starye oshibki, chem mnozhit' novye," *Vek,* 1 September 2000, p. 3; Lyudmila Baklagina, "Oni v koridorakh. Ot kremlya i do Amura my prolozhim vertikal'," *Obshchaya gazeta,* 7 September 2000, p. 7.

45. Relations with government ministries will differ according to the ministry. As Deputy Prime Minister Victor Khristenko explained, there are essentially three different models for ministerial-federal district relations. In some cases, ministries will open new branches in the seven federal districts. In other cases, existing ministerial departments in the capitals of the seven federal districts will serve as the liaison office. And in instances where ministries are not well represented in the provinces, Health and Culture being two such examples, the contact between the federal districts and the ministries will take place in Moscow. "Perestroyka: v kraynem sluchae prezident rassudit," p. 14.

46. Georgiy Osipov, "Pravitel'stvo teryaet vlast'. Predstaviteli prezidenta v federal'nykh okrugakh mogut rasshirit' svoy polnomochiya za schet prem'er-ministra," *Segodnya,* 11 August 2000, p. 1.

47. Shkel', "Ot Moskvy do samykh do okrain. Konstantin Pulikovskiy."

48. Larisa Aydinova, "Taynaya duma Kremlya," *Vek,* 1 January 2001, p. 2.

49. Aleksandr Yurov, "Znakomye vse litsa," *Vremya MN,* 29 December 2000. It should be noted, however, that several of those who did not win had been targeted for removal by Putin and his staff. These included the governors of the Kaliningrad and Ulyanovsk regions, who lost to Kremlin favorites Admiral Vladimir Yegorov and General Vladimir Shamanov. Yegorov and Shamanov join several other general-governors—as opposed to governors-general—as leaders of Russian provinces. Besides the Lebed brothers—the younger actually a colonel rather than a general—one also finds Vladimir Kulakov of the FSB in Voronezh and Boris Gromov in Moscow.

50. Robert Orttung, "The Hard Road to Federal Reform," *Moscow Times,* 28 March 2001.

51. Petr Akopov and Svetlana Babaeva, "Promezhutochnaya cherta. Putin otkazyvaetsiya ot 'osobykh otnosheniy' s kandidatami v gubernatory," *Izvestiya,* 29 September 2000, p. 3.

52. Marina Romanova, "Kogo vybral Kaliningrad?" *Moskovskiy komsomolets,* 20 November 2000, p. 2; and Vladimir Zhukov, "Kreml' pobedil na zapade Rossii," *Kommersant-Daily,* 21 November 2000, p. 2.

53. Konstantin Olen'kov, "Vertikal' narodnoy vlasti. Demokraticheskie vybory v Rossii imeyut istoriyu," *Izvestiya,* 10 January 2001, p. 10.

54. Yelena Kondrateva and Yelena Tregubova, "Gubernator Mikhaylov izvinilsya za anti-semitizm," *Kommersant-Daily,* 16 November 2000, p. 1; Ol'ga Tropkina, "Aleksandr Rutskoy otstupat' ne nameren," *Nezavisimaya gazeta,* 4 November 2000, p. 3; and Roman Arshanskiy and Aleksandr Khinshtein, "Razborki po gubernatorski," *Moskovskiy komsomolets,* 21 November 2000, p. 1.

55. "Nasha Rossiya obretaet sebya," *Krasnaya zvezda,* 6 January 2001, p. 1, which contains a lengthy and revealing interview with Putin.

56. They have also formed coordinating committees of law enforcement representatives in each federal district as a means of reviving federal control in this sector. See Igor' Gugrov, "Polpred Cherkesov vossozdaet vlast' Sovetov," *Kommersant-Daily,* 26 October 2000, p. 2.

57. Yuriy Chernega, "Gubernator Rossel' vynes preduprezhdenie prezidentu," *Kommersant-Daily*, 15 December 2000, p. 2; and Petr Akopov, "Smena khozyaev. Skoro polpredy poluchat real'nuyu vlast' v regionakh," *Izvestiya*, 21 October 2000, p. 1. Governors-general are also emerging as intermediaries and arbiters between rival factions in provincial politics. In Ul'yanovsk, for example, the speaker of the regional assembly appealed to Governor-General Kirienko to create a commission in the province to investigate "gubernatorial sabotage" of legislative activity. It seems that the local governor had encouraged his supporters in the chamber to boycott the legislature's meetings to prevent the adoption of what the speaker regarded as essential legislation. Anna Stryagina, "Dralis', poka ne sravnyalis'," *Nezavisimaya gazeta*, 14 December 2000, p. 4.

58. Aleksey Chernyshev, "V Primor'e prodolzhaetsya fevral'skaya revolyutsiya," *Kommersant-Daily*, 14 February 2001; Evgeniya Lents, "Zachistka Primor'ya. Vladimir Putin ubezhdaet Evgeniya Nazdratenko bol'she ne khodit' v gubernatory," *Segodnya*, 15 February 2001; Oleg Zhunusov, "Svyato mesto. Kreslo gubernatora ne uspeet ostyt'," *Izvestiya*, 7 February 2001; and Yelena Gamayun, "Gubernator sdal—i.o. prinyal," *Moskovskiy Komsomolets*, 7 February 2001.

59. For an introduction to the presidency's provincial affairs subdivisions in the late Yeltsin era, see M. A. Sakhle, "Organizatsionnye formy vzaimodestviya Prezidenta RF s sub'ektami RF," *Zakonodatel'stvo*, no. 6 (1998): 67–75. As the author points out, many presidential bureaus have some responsibilities for center-periphery issues, even if they are not their primary concern. Thus, the head of the State-Legal Administration and Putin protege, Dmitriy Kozak, was assigned the task of bringing provincial legislation in line with the constitution and federal law. "Voloshin razdal portfeli," *Kommersant-Daily*, 21 June 2000; Lyudmila Romanova, "Administratsiya prezidenta opredelila prioritety," *Nezavisimaya gazeta*, 16 June 2000.

60. Kalashnikova, "Sergey Samoylov."

61. For a penetrating portrait of Voloshin, see Dmitriy Pinsker, "Golova administratsii," *Itogi*, 26 June 2000. Despite the consolidation of territorial departments under one roof, not all revisions to the Moscow-based presidential apparatus under Putin have lessened institutional redundancy. There remains in place an Administration of Experts, currently headed by Simon Kordonskiy, which assumes general responsibility for conducting analytical work for the Kremlin and Old Square and for preparing materials for presidential speechwriters. But alongside this institution, separate analytical centers, or departments, continue to function within other presidential structures, most notably within the Main Territorial Administration and the Domestic Policy Administration. It remains to be seen whether, as one presidential source argued, the Administration of Experts will remain focused on more abstract (*kabinetnye*) questions while the analytical departments turn their attention to more practical matters, such as how to handle the transition in Tatarstan as President Mintimer Shaymiev approaches the end of his second—and it was hoped, final—term in office. Although this last question might appear to be a primary concern for the Main Territorial Administration, *Izvestiya* reports that, according to the "logic of the [presidential] apparatus," the issue falls within the realm of the Administration for Domestic Policy. Andrei Kolesnikov, "Staraya ploshchad' obrastaet analitikami," *Izvestiya*, 7 September 2000, p. 3.

62. O polnomochnom predstavitele Prezidenta Rossiyskoy Federatsii v federal'nom okruge, *Sobranie zakonodatel'stva*, no. 20 (2000), st. 2112. It is revealing that in the Central Federal District, Georgiy Poltavchenko appointed as one of his deputies Anton Fedorov, who had served previously as the head of the presidency's Department for Coordinating the Activities of

Presidential Representatives. Alla Barakhova, "Putin podderzhal svoikh polpredov zhivoy siloy," *Kommersant-Daily,* 13 July 2000, p. 2.

63. FAPSI—the Federal Agency for Government Communications and Information Technology—will provide the governors-general secure telephones as well as computer equipment. "O razmeshchenii polnomochnykh predstaviteley Prezidenta RF v federal'nykh okrugakh i sotrudnikov ikh apparatov," *Sobranie zakonodatel'stva,* no. 31 (2000), st. 3257. According to published reports, Vladimir Kozhin, the head of the Administration of Affairs, has promised each governor-general a personal aircraft for his use, an essential perquisite given the frequent flights required to Moscow and the various cities within their own far-flung districts. Denis Babichenko, "Kak nam obustroit' polpredov," *Segodnya,* 9 June 2000.

64. The formation of the State Council brought into the open tensions within the presidency itself between the Main State-Legal Administration and the Main Territorial Administration. Where the former insisted that the State Council would "not be granted any serious powers," Samoylov and the Territorial Administration entertained the idea of granting it responsibilities that had been exercised by the Federation Council. Svetlana Sukhova, "Nuzhny li vlasti novye vlasti. Chto takoe Gossovet, v Kremle kazhdyy ponimaet po-svoemu," *Segodnya,* 3 August 2000, p. 1.

The Main Territorial Administration also plays a role in planning Putin's visits to the provinces, which include a number of upcoming trips to the centers of the new federal districts. See Kalashnikova, "Sergey Samoylov." According to Samoylov, "the task of our Administration is to pull together all the information concerning the locations of his stops on a visit and the themes of the meetings, and transfer this to the first deputy chief of staff, Dmitriy Medvedev, who coordinates the efforts of all agencies in the organization of presidential trips."

65. Voprosy obespecheniya deyatel'nosti apparatov polnomochnykh predstaviteley Prezidenta Rossiyskoy Federatsii v federal'nykh okrugakh, *Sobranie zakonodatel'stva,* no. 26 (2000), st. 2748.

66. O vnesenii izmeneniy i dopolneniy v ukazy Prezidenta RF ot 12 aprelya 1996 g. No 529 "O perechnyakh gosudarstvennykh dolzhnostey federal'noy gosudarstvennoy sluzhby kategoriy "B" i "V" v Administratsii Prezidenta RF i apparate Soveta Bezopasnosti RF' i ot 9 aprelya 1997 g. No 310 'O denezhnom soderzhanii federal'nykh gosudarstvennykh sluzhashchikh," *Sobranie zakonodatel'stva,* no. 22 (2000), st. 2288.

67. It is instructive that, on a visit to St. Petersburg in early August 2000, Putin took along Vladislav Surkov and Aleksandr Abramov for a discussion with the Northwest Federal District's governor-general, Victor Cherkesov. Other participants included Aleksandr Abramov; German Gref, the Minister of Economics; MVD chief Vladimir Rushaylo; Procurator-General Vladimir Ustinov; and the head of the State Customs Committee, Mikhail Banin. Nikolay Poroskov, "Putin na Severo-Zapade," *Vek,* 4 August 2000, p. 2.

68. Marina Kalashnikova, "U polpredov poyavilis' svoi sovety. Novym strukturam otdadut nekotorye funktsii ispolnitel'noy vlasti," *Nezavisimaya gazeta,* 4 August 2000, p. 3.

69. Denis Babichenko and Andrey Kamakin, "Sovetskaya vlast' prikhodit na Dal'niy Vostok," *Segodnya,* 3 August 2000, p. 1; and Andrey Kolesnikov, "Staraya ploshchad' obrastaet analitikami," *Izvestiya,* 7 September 2000, p. 3.

70. See Petr Akopov and Aleksandr Sadchikov, "Final'nyy raund: siloviki ne smogut vytesnit' gubernatorov," *Izvestiya,* 21 December 2000, p. 4. It should be noted that many governors

sought to assert their closeness to Putin during the campaign even if they were not an ally of the Kremlin.

71. In November 2000 a draft decree was circulating in the Kremlin that promised to restrain the autonomy of the governors-general by subordinating them to the presidency's Cadres Department on matters of patronage within their own offices. One highly placed Kremlin official complained that many of the governors-general "had not adapted to their new posts" and were committing "many mistakes, large and small." Nikolay Gul'ko, "Kreml' otkorrektiruet svoikh polpredov," *Kommersant-Daily,* 23 November 2000, p. 2.

72. For the text of this short decree, see "O vnesenii dopolneniy i izmeneniy v Polozhenie o polnomochnom predstavitele Prezidenta RF v federal'nom okruge," *Rossiyskaya gazeta,* 31 January 2001, p. 1. Although it is tempting to see this decree as a personal victory for the incumbent chief of staff, Alexander Voloshin—who at the time appeared to be fighting off attempts by the head of the Security Council, Sergey Ivanov, to expand his political influence over the governors-general—the continuing rumors of Voloshin's early departure from the presidency suggest that Voloshin could take little comfort in his newly acquired powers. Voloshin, it will be recalled, was a carryover from the Yeltsin presidency with numerous friends among the Yeltsin family and numerous adversaries among Putin loyalists.

73. For accounts of the planned downsizing of the Main Territorial Administration, see Larisa Aydinova, "Prorvalo . . . ," *Vek,* 2 February 2001, p. 3; Petr Akopov and Viktoriya Sokolova, "Ukaz ili ne ukaz. Semero zhdut odnogo—novogo opekuna," *Izvestiya,* 31 January 2001, p. 4; and Kaleriya Pukhova, "Reorganizatsiya v administratsii. Utochnena skhema podchineniya polpredov," *Nezavisimaya gazeta,* 30 January 2001, p. 3.

74. Akopov and Sokolova, "Ukaz ili ne ukaz."

75. "Vzaimodeystvie pravitel'stva i polpredov," *St-Peterburgskie vedomosti,* 11 August 2000, p. 1; and Aleksandr Porfir'ev, "Kas'yanovskiy posol. Pravitel'stvo RF otkryvaet posol'stva v federal'nykh okrugakh," *Segodnya,* 5 August 2000, p. 1.

76. Osipov, "Pravitel'stvo teryaet vlast'."

77. Vladimir Bekmetov, "Kas'yanov pochti v otstavke. Prem'er podpisal dokument o sdache polnomochii predstavitelyam prezidenta," *Segodnya,* 17 August 2000, p. 2.

78. Nikolay Poroskov, "Sem' kulakov silovikov," *Vek,* 2 June 2000.

79. Galina Koval'skaya, "Razdelka sushi," *Itogi,* 23 May 2000.

6

Conclusion

Lilia Shevtsova

In this book we have attempted to analyze diverse aspects of the political leadership during the collapse of the Soviet Union and formation of a new Russia. The book compares the rule of Mikhail Gorbachev, Boris Yeltsin, and Vladimir Putin. Moreover, we are trying to evaluate the leadership of these politicians from various points of view, analyzing their goals and the means for attaining these goals, their style of governing, the sources of their influence, and the factors that furthered their activities or complicated them.

The reader will see that the authors sometimes disagree with one another in their evaluations of the leadership of the politicians who have led Russia from communism. In any case, we are accentuating the diverse sides of this leadership. Archie Brown believes that Gorbachev had already become a conscious systemic transformer by 1988. As for Yeltsin, Brown seriously doubts that he deepened the democratic process in post-Soviet Russia. George Breslauer, for his part, emphasizes that Gorbachev and Yeltsin turned out to be successful above all in carrying out their negative goals, that is, in undermining and destroying the old system. But he believes that it is still too soon to draw final conclusions about how well they succeeded in building a new system. Eugene Huskey is very skeptical about the possible consequences of Putin's political-administrative reforms. He does not rule out that, instead of creating a strong state, the reforms could lead to the formation of new centers of influence outside Moscow. As for myself, I emphasize the fact that as of May 2001 Putin did not know how to go beyond the limits of the elected monarchy formed by Yeltsin, which raises doubts about whether the regime can become the basis for a more inclusive and democratic state.

As the book shows, we are dealing here with entirely different political personalities who bear absolutely no resemblance to one another either by character or temperament. Furthermore, they have had different aims and have acted in differing social and geopolitical circumstances. Gorbachev attempted to become a reformer of socialism and strove to make that system of government more humane and closer to Western values. Yeltsin, as it once seemed and still seems to many, including perhaps Yeltsin himself, played the role of a revolutionary who shattered the previous state and tried to erect, albeit without any kind of plan, a new Russia. Putin is trying to escape the chaos that Yeltsin brought about and become a kind of stabilizer by strengthening the state and bringing social order. Consider also that Gorbachev governed at a time of rising social activism, when society had become ripe for fundamental changes. Yeltsin began to govern at a moment when the democratic wave was subsiding and left in an atmosphere of discontent and the retreat of people into their private lives. Putin came to power on a wave of nostalgia for the past and a longing for order and an "iron hand." If we lined up these politicians in a row, we would see how dissimilar they are in their goals, in their style, and in the consequences of their actions. We would see how different their teams, their behavior, and the makeup of their political and social base of support are. Despite the fact that Putin was chosen by Yeltsin to be his successor, Putin presents a different type of pragmatic, even technocratic leadership, and is often perceived in Russia not so much as a leader, but rather as a function of leadership. Moreover, in order to gain his own legitimacy he is forced not only to distance himself from his "godfather," but also to dismantle elements of his regime.

Nonetheless, there are things that draw these leaders together. Gorbachev, Yeltsin, and Putin all acted and act by intuition, following their feelings and obeying their instincts. They are all, regardless of their various political signatures, rather intuitive leaders. Perhaps this is a consequence of their having to function under conditions of a continuing transitional period, in the absence of rules of the game recognized by all and of strong institutions. Objectively, they are forced to improvise, mix up principles, experiment, and sound out opportunities for themselves and society. This continues to be reflected in their spontaneous actions, unexpected upheavals, often arbitrary and unpredictable policies, and political developments as a whole. But what is important is that not one of them has made it his goal to create a system of independent institutions with separate spheres of responsibility or has tried to attain a consensus in society on Russia's future path of development. Quite often they have not informed the people of their intentions.

All three have encountered, and Putin continues to encounter, unintended consequences, first of all because they obey their instincts and do not attempt to follow a thoughtful strategy based on distinct principles. Thus, while clearly attempting to reform the old system, Gorbachev by force of his own will brought about destructive elements, and it was he who pushed the former state and system of values toward destruction. Having pulled out one card, he caused a collapse of the house of cards and, without expecting it himself, became a destroyer. Trying to become a revolutionary, close the books on communism, and bury the old state, Yeltsin nonetheless gave birth to a destructive paradigm of monolithic power and brought back elements of autocracy, albeit an elected one, to Russia. Trying to strengthen the unraveling state and establish order, Putin harked back to the Soviet period and borrowed methods and sources of support from it. He apparently did not realize that without the resources of the armed forces and given a pluralistic society, returning to a vertical power is impossible. Furthermore, the mechanism of a "transmission belt" devised by him is a vulnerable construction. It might not collapse, but it will inevitably push society toward stagnation and lead it to another dead end.

Still other traits tie these leaders closely together. After all, each belonged to the Soviet elite, however different their generations. Hence it is difficult not to see in their behavior the same suspicion of independent institutions, inability to fully understand when opponents are right and to reach agreements with them, distrust of any opposition, behind-the-scenes methods of decision making, and reliance on the bureaucracy as the main structural source of support. An exaggerated faith in the state, rather than the individual, and efforts to turn the state into the main instrument of progress and modernization are also characteristic of all of them. I have the feeling that only Gorbachev has reevaluated this approach, and only after he ceased being a ruler. Having begun with constructive goals, both Gorbachev and Yeltsin ended up as politicians who thought above all about their own survival. Unfortunately, Putin too provides reasons to suspect that, for him, consolidating power could become a goal in itself.

All these leaders were prepared to be victims of divisiveness and internal conflicts, regardless of the degree to which they understood them. They were forced to carry out antisystemic changes at moments when they were not prepared internally. Perhaps only Putin is still avoiding such torturous division and acts more according to his own views than previous leaders, for his aim—bringing order to the country—does not yet demand that he take radical steps. But he has been forced to appeal to various sections of the population, and must continue to do so if he wants to preserve stability.

But most important is that all these leaders have had to survive—Putin still has to survive—the extremely difficult test of their ability to move society away from paradigms of development that are traditional for Russia. This has always included a monolithic, indivisible power with authority vested in a single subject, the existence of society in the framework of a superstate, and the belief in a "special" path of development for Russia. Gorbachev and Yeltsin came close to a way out of this paradigm. In some ways and at certain times they even broke away from it. But they did not succeed in renouncing it entirely, not only because of their views and limitations, but also because of the limits imposed by the people, the majority of whom still could not fully accept the principles and formulas of liberal democracy.

During Gorbachev's and Yeltsin's periods of rule, Russian society tore itself away only from the communist-Soviet shell of this paradigm. But the beliefs that had been formulated over the centuries, along with traditions, ways of thinking, forms of behavior, and means of survival, were preserved and were simply infused into new institutions borrowed from liberal-democratic models. More than 70 percent of Russian citizens polled continue to believe in the uniqueness of their country and its "special path" and consider that the Western model of liberal democracy is not suitable for Russia. With Putin's accession to power, the people's belief in Russia's special path has become even stronger, even as this belief is set against the background of all the disappointments and dashed hopes that occurred over the past ten years. Moreover, Putin would never have come to power were it not for this yearning in society to go backward, this nostalgia for the past and for old methods of surviving. Now Putin is trying to conduct a new experiment and forge a synthesis of the Russian autocratic paradigm with the requirements of modernization. It remains to be seen how far this is possible and whether he will manage, within the limits of this experiment, to preserve stability and stimulate economic development. Doing so is a very difficult, if not impossible, task. It cannot be ruled out that the failure of current attempts to prolong the existence in Russia of undivided power—of the single-subject, autocratic leadership, notwithstanding all the trappings of democratic legitimacy—and the efforts to preserve Russia's superpower role in the world will bring a quicker end to illusions about Russia's exclusiveness, which has done much to prevent it from being included once and for all in Western civilization.

However, it was not Putin who began the experiment of combining Western values and rules of the game with traditional Russian forms of authority; Gorbachev and Yeltsin did. It was they who began to move Russia toward Europe, while at the same time trying to preserve Russian traditions and identity. This experiment resulted in the formation of a rather strange political hybrid, mixed economic relations, and the development of an immense "gray area" of vital activities of both the authorities and society. It was precisely this gray area into which both the authorities and the economy retreated when they could not entirely fit within the framework of civilized liberal-democratic relations. Gorbachev, Yeltsin, and Putin each balanced in his own way, of course, elements of Westernization and Russian traditionalism, change and continuity, and, no less important, revolution and stability. The very process under all these leaders of seeking the means to both move forward and preserve the past was spontaneous and involved much groping for answers, often under the influence of the imagination or character of one or another leader at a particular moment and of his vision of the future. Unfortunately, they often perceived any setback or failure not as a reason to seek other innovative solutions, but as a signal to turn back to an already familiar and customary mechanism.

Gorbachev was prepared to open up the country to Europe, above all in the sphere of international relations, yet he was very cautious when it came to decisively casting off the old system. In the final analysis, at the end of his rule Gorbachev tried to halt the revolutionary collapse that he himself had caused but could not control. Moreover, his attempt to prevent this collapse in 1990–1991, when he clearly lagged behind the demands of the democratic wing of society, only hastened his own fall.

Yeltsin continued to break with the past and sided with Western rules of the game in the field of economics, having given young reformers, headed by Gaidar, the opportunity to begin market therapy. But at the same time, when he began to sense resistance—on the part of both the elite and society—to such rapid changes, he began to gradually move backward to traditional monolithic forms of authority and monarchical manners. In essence, Yeltsin ended up a typical conservative, who is concerned only with preserving power and its succession.

Putin was faced with a choice between preserving continuity with the Yeltsin regime and its politics of connivance and breaking with those politics. At first, Putin chose to make the break, but he also soon began to waver, indeed not even because he encountered resistance, but because he did not decide in which direction to move further. The very break that Putin attempted to make in the middle of 2000 was not in the direction of Westernization but toward a return to a more severe type of elected monarchy.

At the time this book was being written, Putin was still trying to put off making a final choice between a Western and a traditional Russian paradigm of development, mixing elements of both in his politics. But his wavering and use of great-power rhetoric pull him backward to Russian conservatism, which is absolutely alien to Western conservatism and means above all a return to traditions of state regulation and monolithic power. However, at the same time, one has the impression that he senses the limits of this traditionalism. At least he is clearly resisting attempts, for now, to push him toward reproducing Soviet models of development. In any case, despite the increased suspicion of the West within the Russian ruling circles and the prevalence of a Cold War-type atmosphere in Moscow-Washington relations in early 2001, Putin's Russia by the most important indicators has still continued to move in the direction of Western values.

Gorbachev and Yeltsin share the trait that they were forced to fight against Russia's traditional domination by the bureaucracy. Gorbachev made the first break in destroying the *nomenklatura* as an administrative sector integrating the Soviet state and filling the role of a systemic condition for the existence of that state. Yeltsin went further by including skilled functionaries in the system and trying through elections to get rid of the tutelage of the bureaucracy. True, he could not, perhaps did not know how, and maybe even did not want to trust the people. Instead of relying on self-government for support, he turned to a new tsarist court and encouraged the establishment of a Russian oligarchy, trying to use it as a counterweight in his relations with the machinery of state.

By striving to build a vertical power structure and rationalize Yeltsin's tsarist model, Putin essentially cast his lot with the federal bureaucracy, thus in many ways refusing to take the Yeltsin line. But gradually we see signs that he is starting to see he could become hostage to his base. "What is distressing?" he asked himself in March 2001. His answer: "There is one problem that truly cannot but lead to sad thoughts—it is very hard to fight with the bureaucracy."[1] Now, however, the problem for Putin is how to free himself from the embrace of the bureaucracy, which he himself strengthened and continues to strengthen. Who can he rely on for support in society, especially if he plans to further pursue a policy of centralization and limit local initiative and elements of opposition? This is truly a challenge facing Putin and the country, one to which the president cannot yet respond.

To what degree are Gorbachev, Yeltsin, and Putin unique if we put them in the context of world transformational history? Some of the leadership traits we see in their activities appear in the activities of other transformational leaders. The vacillations of Gorbachev, a man who belonged to the old system but found within himself the resolve to leave it, were understood, of course, by Adolfo Suarez, who, as part of the old power structure, began the withdrawal from Francoism in Spain. It should be noted, however, that Suarez managed to go further than Gorbachev in creating new rules of the game, which the Soviet president due to different circumstances was unable to institutionalize. Moreover, one can see in Yeltsin's activities many traits that are characteristic of a regime that Guillermo O'Donnell once called "delegative democracy." O'Donnell wrote that such democracy "rests on the premise that whoever wins the election to the presidency is thereby entitled to govern as he or she sees fit."[2] One can also see in Yeltsin's activities, during various periods of his rule, traits of the Argentinean president Carlos Menem and the Peruvian president Alberto Fujimori. Elements of patrimonialism and nepotism, which prevailed in the rule of the aging Yeltsin, are part of any stagnating or personal regime, and Russia in this sense has not discovered a new phenomenon.

For now it is difficult to place Putin in comparative context, primarily because he has not put forward a definite image and indeed tries to avoid defining the contours of his leadership, incorporating instead several hybrid traits. Putin clearly is transforming the system of elected monarchy formed by Yeltsin, shunning its charismatic and game-like character, and leaning toward a more technocratic and restrained leadership. But it still remains to be seen whether the bureaucratic and coercive basis will prevail in his activities or, if not, the extent to which he will return to the tactics of Yeltsinism. Perhaps Putin will decide to move beyond the framework of elected monarchy. For the time being, there is no basis for such a conclusion. But the political life of Russia remains very fluid and unpredictable. For now, the popular comparison made in Russia between the Putin regime and that of de Gaulle, who was also once called an elected or republican monarch,[3] is unwarranted. During de Gaulle's time in France, there existed a developed system of political relations, including an independent parliament and a government more independent than in Russia. Moreover, the multiparty system and pro-presidential party in France were independent of the president and were not formed by him, as was the case in Russia.

Despite a whole series of analogies that could be drawn between the activities of Gorbachev, Yeltsin, Putin, and other transformational leaders, what sets the rule of Russian politicians apart from many others in transitional societies is above all the maintenance of a personal leadership that rests in the post-Soviet era on the union of political power and money. In its extreme form, this fusion has found expression in many of the sultan-like regimes that arose in several former Soviet republics of Central Asia and the Caucasus. Compared with those regimes, the new powers and leadership in Russia have truly moved in the direction of Western, Roman-European traditions of authority, although they have not acquired their logic.

Russian transformational leadership is clearly moving in a direction that is increasingly dramatic. The drama lies not in the style and behavior of the leader but in the challenges before the country and the authorities. In fact, despite all the significant changes under Gorbachev's and Yeltsin's rule, it was much easier for them to fulfill their function as destroyers of the previous system because it was possible to eliminate one element of the system—the monopoly of the Communist Party—and cause a domino effect.

Putin, in contrast, must now play the role of consolidator, moving society away from a state of permanent revolution, constant shake-ups of functionaries, and periodic crises (which Yeltsin was incapable of mastering). But in order to play such a role, Putin must decide what it is precisely that he is trying to consolidate—the mixed system and hybrid polity that Yeltsin left him? It turns out that consolidating such a system is impossible because it will provoke, on its own, internal conflicts and crises. Then perhaps will he begin moving in the direction of a liberal-democratic system of power and a more open society? For this, he would have to make several breakthroughs, including structural reforms for which neither he, the ruling elite, nor a significant part of society is prepared. Indeed, Putin gained support because he guaranteed order and stability above all. Then will Putin perhaps take it upon himself to turn back abruptly toward traditionalism? He has taken several steps in this direction but evidently came to understand that consolidating society and the system on the basis of traditionalism is also impossible. In the federal capital there is neither the desire nor the coercive and ideological mechanisms for doing so.

Therefore, the role of Putin is very dramatic: whatever he may feel or think, there are no resources for turning Russia back, and the country neither wants nor is ready for a more distinct movement forward toward liberalism. Putin may thus turn out to be yet another transitional leader who has again not succeeded in bringing the country out of its first phase of transformation and setting it on the path of orderly development. He might not succeed above all because, in the society itself, there is still no consensus over the past, present, and future.

Of course, given that the country finds itself between systems and a strong force for moving in any one direction is absent, a politics of imitation is entirely possible as a means of avoiding the resolution of problems and a means of survival. This could involve the imitation of strong leadership, the imitation of democracy, the imitation of the politics of a "firm hand," and the imitation of action and political will. For some, Putin is entirely capable of more or less successfully imitating a kind of Russian Pinochet. In the eyes of others he could imitate de Gaulle. One gets the impression that, by trying to put off major decisions, Putin has already begun to imitate his responses to the challenges that he himself and the country now face. But it is obvious that this politics of imitation has its limits and can only make the problems constantly being put off more acute.

The number of common systemic pitfalls and tendencies in the activities of Gorbachev, Yeltsin, and Putin, the basis of which is a weak institutionalized system of power, does not mean, however, that the model of leadership in Russia has not undergone substantial changes in the course of parting with communism and entering a period of noncommunist development. Albeit cautiously and looking back, Gorbachev nonetheless opened the door for political and ideological pluralism, the legitimization of authority through elections, and free enterprise. He acted on the principle of decompression, gradually emancipating society. While doing so he changed the form and style of ruling the country, desacralizing authority, uncovering its secrets, and making the very process of governing the country transparent.

For Yeltsin, open struggle and conflict became entirely natural, and in this sense he made a break with the Soviet political style of conformity. He was unable, however, to master the art of making a pact and creating consensus, and constantly resorted to the traditional Soviet tactics of political bartering and intrigues within the state apparatus. But it is remarkable that, under Yeltsin, Russia strengthened the new mechanism of legitimizing power through elections. Both the people and the ruling elite came to understand that all other means of fighting for and holding on to power had exhausted themselves.

Despite the fact that Putin is not accustomed to democratic mechanisms and does not feel comfortable in public politics, with its many unknowns and indefiniteness, he could hardly return the country to its former isolation and hermetically sealed authority. There are already doubts that Putin is able to build a new authoritarian vertical chain of command, which would be proof of the country's movement toward decentralization of power and pluralism, which would also force the model of leadership to evolve, becoming more flexible and less authoritarian.

There is some basis for very guarded optimism concerning the future. Whether he wants to or not, President Putin will have to confront the fact that, having inherited from Gorbachev and Yeltsin a country with a disorienting, faith-shattering nostalgia for a past, quiet life, now he presides over 15 percent of the population that is ready to live under a liberal democracy, drawing closer to the West. Is this percentage too many or too few people? It is surely enough to sustain in society a stimulus to reform. And this section of the population could become a strong base of support for the leader if he decides to transform the country more fundamentally in a Westernizing direction. This section of society could also turn out to be a great obstacle if he goes the opposite way.

Notes

1. *Izvestiya,* 22 March 2001.

2. Guillermo O'Donnell, "Delegative Democracy," *Journal of Democracy* 5, no. 1 (January 1994): 59–62.

3. See Ezra N. Suleiman, "Presidential Government in France," in *Presidents and Prime Ministers,* ed. Richard Rose and Ezra Suleiman (Washington, D.C.: American Enterprise Institute for Public Research, 1980), p. 97.

Index

Abramov, Alexander, 130
Abramovich, Roman, 103, 111n48
Acheson, Dean, 64
Afanasyev, Mikhail, 134
Afghanistan, 55
Aganbegyan, Abel, 30
Andreyeva, Nina, 14
Andropov, Yury, 1, 17
Aron, Leon, 25, 65n10
Aydinova, Larisa, 127

Baltic states, 23–24, 38, 60
Berezovsky, Boris, 104
Blat, 16
Boldin, Valery, 13
Brakov, Yegveny, 13
Brazauskas, Algirdas-Mikolas, 38
Breslauer, George, vii, 7–8, 45–66, 143, 161
Brezhnev, Leonid, 2, 5, 17, 32–33, 43n54, 43n56, 45, 52
Brown, Archie, vii, ix, 1–9, 11–43, 143, 161
Burns, James MacGregor, 6
Bush (George W.) administration, viii

Capitalism, 17; Gorbachev administration reforms and, 16; Yeltsin administration reforms and, 37
Carr, E. H., 65n11
Central European countries, 20, 21
Chebrikov, Viktor, 14, 31
Chechnya/Chechen war, 25, 91, 93, 110n34, 119
Cherkesov, Viktor, 120, 124
Chernenko, Konstantin, 1, 6, 17, 43n56, 56–57
Chernomyrdin, Viktor, 83, 118
Chernyaev, Anatoly, 13, 21, 22, 27, 41n25
Chubais, Anatoly, 16, 30, 31, 32, 84, 116, 117, 118
Civil liberties, 62, 69; Gorbachev administration, 53; Putin administration, 101
Coal miners' strikes, 56
Cold War, ending of, 17–18, 20, 37–38, 53
Comecon, 21
Communist Party of Russian Republic, 81; formation of, 24; Putin admin-

istration and, 5, 95, 96; Yeltsin administration and, 86–87, 88

Communist Party of the Soviet Union (CPSU), 8n2; Gorbachev and, 32, 35; in pluralization of Soviet political system, 13; International Department, 21-22, 41n25; as political institution, 2; post-Stalinist, 1–3; power of general secretary, 2–3; Yeltsin and, 26, 28, 33–34, 36, 57

Congress of the International Council for Central and East European Studies, ix

Conquest, Robert, 23–24

Constitution of *1993*, 35, 62, 76, 107n11; legislative power structure in, 114; prospects for revision, 135n22; provincial constitutions and, 126, 134n3, 136n32; regional relations under, 120

Council of Local Government, 116

Counterfactual analysis, 48–51

Coup attempt of *1991*, 4, 15

CPSU. *See* Communist Party of the Soviet Union

Criminal justice, 119–20

Dallin, Alex, 25

Debré, Michel, 108n18

De Gaulle, Charles, 108n18

Democratic processes: current trends in Russia, 148; election of *2000*, 90–92; federal district administration and, 123, 127–28; in former Soviet states, 39; future of Putin administration, 150–51, 152; Gorbachev administration reforms, 13–14, 22, 23–24, 25, 36, 53; market reform and, 69; Putin commitment to, 5, 96; Russia as hybrid system, 16, 36–37, 75, 76–80, 103, 147–48; Yeltsin administration reforms, 36–37, 60, 68–70, 73–75, 76, 78–80, 87–88, 108n16, 143;

Yeltsin's commitment to, 31–32, 69–70

Democratic Russia, 56

Dobrynin, Anatoly, 21, 22

Drachevsky, Leonid, 123, 137n39

Duma, 29; Putin administration relations, 5, 96, 97; Yeltsin administration relations, 31–32, 49, 86–87

Dyachenko, Tatyana, 26, 85–86

Eastern European countries, 53, 55–56; dissolution of Soviet state, 20–22, 38–39

Economic functioning: crisis of *1998*, 63, 86, 115; democratic reform and, 69; feudal characteristics, 16, 80, 81; future prospects, 16; Gorbachev administration reforms, 15–16, 35–36, 37, 49, 53, 54; hybrid system, 16; "partial reform equilibrium," 16, 17, 37; political interest groups, 82; provincial governance and, 126–27; Putin administration reforms, 95, 103, 105; transition from command economy, 15–17, 30, 53; transition to market economy, 15, 16, 30, 79; Yeltsin administration reforms, 4, 16–17, 30–31, 37, 49, 60, 66n24, 70

Elites: in breakup of Soviet Union, 24; fragmentation, 74, 84, 98; in Putin administration, 98, 104; in regional relations, 113–14, 120; in Yeltsin administration, 88. *See also* Nomenklatura; Oligarchs

English, Robert, 18–19

Ericson, Richard E., 16

Estonia, 24, 39

Ethnic conflict, 22

Falin, Valentin, 21, 22

Fatherland-All Russia movement, 94

Federation Council, 96, 114, 135n19

Fedorov, Boris, 84

Fedorov, Nikolay, 135n22

Foreign policy: ending of Cold War, 17–18, 37–38; Gorbachev administration, 17–20, 21–22, 37–38, 53, 55–56; Yeltsin administration, 18, 37, 38–39, 59

FSB, 119, 124, 125

Future prospects, vii–viii; constitutional revision, 135n22; economic system, 16; evaluation of Gorbachev, 64; evaluation of Yeltsin, 64; federal district governance, 132–34; Putin administration, 7, 98–107, 143–44, 146–47, 149–51, 152; Putin administration goals, 4–5; Yeltsin legacy, 90

Gaidar, Yegor, 16, 30, 31, 83, 84

Gazprom, 103

Germany, 21–22

Glasnost, 13, 55

Gorbachev, Mikhail: in 1996 election, 29; personal qualities, 18–19, 26–27, 30, 56–57. *See also* Gorbachev general secretaryship

Gorbachev, Raisa, 19, 29, 43n49

Gorbachev Foundation, 26, 27

Gorbachev general secretaryship, 7–8; attempted coup d'état, 3–4, 15; counterfactual justification of policy, 48, 49; disengagement from Eastern Europe, 20–22; in dissolution of Soviet state, 3, 11–12, 22–24, 31, 36, 37–39; economic reforms in, 15–16, 35–36, 37, 53; in ending of Cold War, 17–18, 20; foreign policy formulation, 17–20, 21–22, 37–38, 55–56; historical significance, 2–3, 4–6, 39–40, 64; influences on, 13, 30, 31; leadership style, 26–27, 56–57, 144–45; in pluralization of Soviet political system, 3, 12–15, 52–53, 151; political effectiveness, 7, 33, 35; political institutions supporting, 32–33; political opponents of, 3–4,

14, 33; public opinion, 28–29; reform goals, 12, 13–14, 16, 36, 45, 46–47, 144; reform outcomes, 52–54, 64, 147, 148; relations with legislature, 29; social pressure for change in, 55, 56, 144; transformational leadership in, 14, 21, 35–40, 51–57, 143, 149; Yeltsin and, 12, 24, 26, 43n56, 56, 57. *See also* Gorbachev, Mikhail

Gorbenko, Leonid, 128

Gosplan, 17, 41n15

Gossnab, 17, 41n15

Governors, 114–15, 121, 128–29

Grachev, Andrey, 3–4, 24, 41n25

Gromyko, Andrey, 14, 17

Grósz, Károly, 20

Hellman, Joel, 16

Holmes, Leslie, ix

Hough, Jerry, 22, 65n10

Hungary, 20

Huskey, Eugene, vii, 113–141, 143, 161

Hybrid political system, 16, 36–37, 75, 76–80, 103, 147–48

Institutional structure and function: CPSU as political institution, 2; determinants of, 7; dissolution of Soviet state, 3; federal district administration, 121–26; in Gorbachev administration, 32–33, 61; provincial politics, 115–18, 119; Putin administration reforms, 101, 115–18; to support economic reform, 79; transformational leadership, 51–52; Yeltsin administration challenges, 58–59, 73–74; Yeltsin administration reforms, 33–34, 60–61, 63, 80–83, 114

Interest group politics: creation of private economic interests, 17; in Putin administration, 99–100, 101–2, 103–4; in Yeltsin administration, 82, 84

Ivanov, Sergey, 132

Kádár, János, 20
Kalashnikova, Marina, 131
Karl, Terry Lynn, 108n16
Kazantsev, Viktor, 125, 137n39
KGB, 15, 31, 93
Khasbulatov, Ruslan, 30–31
Kholmskaya, Irina, 114
Khristenko, Viktor, 138n45
Khrushchev, Nikita, 1–2, 3, 8n2, 45
Kirienko, Sergey, 83, 123, 124
Kissinger, Henry, 65–66n22
Korzhakov, Alexander, 12, 27–28, 31, 85
Kryuchkov, Vladimir, 15, 31
Kulakov, Anatoly, 32
Kursk submarine event, 96–97, 111n45

Latvia, 39
Latyshev, Petr, 127, 129
Leadership style: challenges in Russia, 67–68, 71–74; common features of post-Soviet leaders, 144–46; counterfactual analysis of outcomes, 48–51; during dissolution of Soviet state, 3–4; effective, 6–7, 46–47, 49–50; Gorbachev's, 26–27, 56–57, 144–45; influence of, on state functioning, 1; methods of evaluation, 45–48, 68–69; in post-Soviet Russia, 150–52; Putin's, 5, 90, 93–94, 95, 97–98, 144–45; in Soviet system, 1–3; transactional, 6, 7; transforming/transformational, 6–7, 11–12, 35–40, 51–57, 71, 149–50; Yeltsin's, 26, 27–28, 68–71, 82–83, 85–86, 144–45
Legislative branch of Russian government: campaign of *1999*, 94; executive branch relations, 29, 75–76, 86–87; governors in, 114–15, 121; provisions of constitution of *1993*, 114; Putin administration and, 5,

96; Yeltsin administration and, 29, 114. *See also* Duma
Lenin, 3, 6, 8n2, 9n12
Ligachev, Yegor, 13, 14–15, 36, 57
Lithuania, 24, 38, 39
Lobov, Oleg, 31
Lukyanov, Anatoly, 14
Luzhkov, Yury, 94

Mamut, Alexander, 111n48
Maslyukov, Yury, 86
Mass media: Putin administration and, 5, 98, 101; Yeltsin administration and, 34
Matlock, Jack, 13
McFaul, Michael, 107n10, 108n16
Medvedev, Vadim, 21, 31
Mikhaylov, Alexander, 128
Military establishment: Gorbachev administration and, 32–33; Putin administration and, 5, 101; Russian federal districts and, 123
Molotov, Vyacheslav, 48
Moral leadership, 6

Nationalism, Yeltsin administration and, 63
Nazdratenko, Yevgeny, 123, 129–30
Nepotism, 85–86
New thinking, 18, 23, 55
Nikonov, Viktor, 14
Nineteenth Party Conference, 13, 14, 20, 28
Nomenklatura, 2; Gorbachev reforms and, 53; modern Soviet leadership, 22, 92–93

O'Donnell, Guillermo, 8–9n4, 108n16, 149
Oligarchs, 34, 84–85, 95–96, 99, 109n26, 111n48, 148
Orttung, Robert, 127

Palazchenko, Pavel, 18, 27
People's Deputy party, 96

Perestroika, 13, 55
Petrakov, Nikolay, 30
Politburo, Gorbachev and, 13, 14, 29, 56–57
Political functioning: center-periphery relations, 116; challenges for Putin administration, 99–107; counterfactual analysis, 48–51; economic interest groups in, 82; effective leadership style, 6–7, 46–47, 49–50; election of *2000*, 90–94; executive–legislative relations, 29; future of provincial governance, 126–34; Gorbachev administration, 35; leadership evaluation methods, 45–48; opposition to Gorbachev reforms, 3–4, 33; perceived role of political opposition, 91–92; pluralization of Soviet system, 12–15, 36–37, 52–53; political crimes, 119–20; Putin administration, 5, 95, 97–98; Russian cultural history, 76–77, 79–80, 113; of Russian oligarchs, 84–85; social pressure for change in Gorbachev administration, 55, 56; transformational leadership, 51–52; Yeltsin administration, 33–34, 35, 62–63, 69–71, 88. *See also* Leadership style; Power structure
Poltavchenko, Georgy, 125, 128
Popov, Gavril, 34
Poroskov, Nikolay, 133
Potanin, Vladimir, 109n26
Power structure: Gorbachev administration, 14, 52, 53, 148; governors in, 114–15; nonsystemic, 80–81; position of general secretary of CPSU, 2–3, 8n2; in post-Stalinist Soviet Union, 1–3, 8n3; prime minister in, 86–87; provincial governance, 120, 121–34; provisions of constitution of *1993*, 114; Putin administration, 5, 95–96, 100–101, 115–16, 121, 148–49; regional

relations, 81, 113–15, 117; Russian political culture, 76–77, 78–80; Yeltsin administration, 26, 33–34, 49, 75–80, 81, 82, 86–87, 148, 151–52. *See also* Political functioning
Primakov, Yevgeny, 83, 86, 87, 91, 94, 109n30
Prime ministers, in Yeltsin administration, 83, 86–87
Privatization, 15–16; Yeltsin reforms, 17, 37
Provincial and local government: current power structure, 121–32; democratic processes in, 123, 127–28; economic policy, 126–27; federal ministries and, 138n45; future challenges, 132–34; Main Territorial Administration, 130–31, 132, 140n64; political appointments in, 128–30; in Putin administration, 115–16, 119–34; in Yeltsin administration, 113–15, 116, 117
Public opinion, 110n33, 111n43, vii–viii; of Chechen war, 91, 110n34; development of opposition to Soviet state, 3; on dissolution of Soviet state, 42n39; in election of Putin, 90–94; future of Russia in, 146; of Gorbachev administration, 28–29; *Kursk* submarine event in, 97, 111n45; of Putin administration, 97, 98–99, 100, 101, 104–5, 110nn35–36, 111n48; on role of political opposition, 91–92; Russian self-perception and, 62–63, 146; social pressure for change in Gorbachev administration, 55, 56; of Yeltsin administration, 28, 63
Pulikovsky, Konstantin, 123, 127, 129–30, 131
Putin, Vladimir, 83; personal qualities, 93; in Yeltsin administration, 118
Putin administration, 8; antecedents to institutional reforms, 115–18;

conditions in Russia at start of, 4, 144; economic reforms, 95, 103, 105; election of, 90–94; future prospects, 7, 143–44, 146–47, 149–51, 152, viii; goals, 4–5, 93–94, 95, 100, 110nn39, 146–47; interest group politics, 99–100, 101–2, 103–4; *kontrol'* bureaucracy, 119, 124, 131; *Kursk* event, 96–97; leadership style, 5, 90, 93–94, 95, 97–98, 144–45; legislative branch relations, 96; media relations, 5, 98, 101; military establishment and, 101; power structure, 95–96, 100–101, 115–16, 148–49; provincial and local government, 115–16, 119–34; public opinion, 97, 98–99, 100, 101, 104–5, 110nn35–36, 111n48; Yeltsin legacy and, 90, 94, 95, 103, 144. *See also* Putin, Vladimir

Rakhimov, Murtaz, 129
Reagan administration, 17, 18
Rossel, Eduard, 129
Russia: in breakup of Soviet Union, 23–25; development of hybrid democratic governance, 36–37, 76–80, 103, 147–48; leadership challenges, 67–68, 71–74; political culture, 76–77, 79–80, 108nn19–20, 113, 146; post-Soviet leadership, 150–52; provincial and local government, 113–15, 116, 117; regional relations, 24, 38–39, 113–15, 120; state symbols, 99–100
Russian Federation, 25, 47
Rutskoy, Alexander, 30–31, 128
Ryzhkov, Nikolay, 31

Sakharov, Andrey, 9n6, 71
Sakwa, Richard, 108n16, 109n23
Samoylov, Yevgeny, 130
Schapiro, Leonard, 2

Schmitter, Philippe, 8–9n4, 108n16
Schultz, George, 18, 20
Schumpeter, Joseph, 51
Shakhnazarov, Georgy, 21, 26, 42–43n41
Shamanov, General Vladimir, 138n49
Shaymiev, Mintimer, 139n61
Shatalin, Stanislav, 30
Shevardnadze, Eduard, 17, 20, 21, 31
Shevtsova, Lilia, vii, ix, 67–111, 135n22, 143–152, 162
Šimon, Bohumil, 43n54
Solomentsev, Mikhail, 14
Solzhenitsyn, Alexander, 9n6
Soviet state: development of opposition, 3; disengagement from Eastern Europe, 20–22; economic reforms, 15–17; Gorbachev reform goals, 11–12; leadership during dissolution of, 3–4, 20–25, 36, 37–39; pluralization of political system, 12–15, 36–37; possibility of preserving, 22–24; power structure, 1–3, 8n3
Stalin, 1, 2, 6, 8n2, 9n12, 47
State Committee for the State of Emergency, 31
State Council, 121
Stepashin, Sergey, 83
Stoner-Weiss, Kathryn, 134n5
Suarez, Adolfo, 149
Sukhodrev, Viktor, 26–27
Svyazy, 16

Taylor, A. J. P., 65n11
Terrorism, 91
Thompson, E. P., 65n11
Tikhomirov, Lev, 76
Trade rules, 115
Turovsky, R. F., 114, 116, 118

Udmurtiya, 116, 117–18
Union of Rightist Forces, 96
Union Republics, 22–25, 38–39
United States, 17–18

Unity party, 94, 96
Uskorenie, 13
Ustinov, Dmitry, 17

Voloshin, Alexander, 130, 139n61, 141n72
Vorotnikov, Vitaly, 14

Warsaw Pact, 21
Western perception: ending of Cold War, 17; Russian political spectrum, 14
Wyman, Matthew, 42n39

Yabloko, 96
Yakovlev, Alexander, 13, 17, 21, 27, 31
Yegorov, Admiral, 128, 138n49
Yeltsin, Boris: in Communist Party, 26, 28; in dissolution of Soviet state, 4, 11–12, 24–25, 37–39; in ending of Cold War, 18; Gorbachev and, 12, 24, 26, 43n56, 56, 57; historical significance, 57–58; personal qualities, 26, 27–28, 30; in pluralization of Soviet political system, 13; political career, 28, 57–58; political ideology, 36, 70, 83; political skills, 18, 69, 70–71
Yeltsin administration, 7–8; attempted coup of 1991 and, 4; center-periphery relations in, 116; commitment to democracy, 31–32, 69–70; conditions in Russia at start of, 58, 73, 144; constitution of 1993, 76, 114; counterfactual justification of policy, 48–49; democratic reforms,

68–70, 73–75, 76, 77, 78–80, 87–88, 108n16, 143; economic reforms in, 16–17, 30–31, 37, 60, 66n24, 70; election of 1996, 29, 31–32; foreign policy formulations, 18, 37; historical significance, 4–5, 5–6, 64; influences on, 30–32, 82–83; institution-building in, 61; interest groups, 82, 84; leadership style, 26, 27–28, 68–71, 82–83, 85–86, 144–45; liberal technocrats in, 83–84; media relations, 34; oligarchs in, 84–85; outcomes, 4, 59–63, 64, 68–69, 88–90, 144, 147–48, 151–52; political effectiveness, 7, 35; political ideology, 83; political institutions supporting, 33–34, 83; political rhetoric, 62–63; prime ministers, 83, 86–87; provincial and local government, 113–15, 116, 117; public opinion, 28, 63, 109n30; Putin administration and, 91, 92, 94, 103, 144; Putin in, 118; reform goals, 45, 46–47, 57, 58–59, 70, 74–75; regional relations in, 38–39, 81, 113–15, 117; relations with legislature, 29, 49, 75–76, 86–87; resignation, 87; Russian self-perception and, 62–63; transformational leadership in, 17, 35, 71. *See also* Yeltsin, Boris
Yerin, Viktor, 26

Zakaria, Fareed, 108n16
Zaslavskaya, Tatyana, 30

Contributors

George W. Breslauer is Chancellor's Professor of Political Science and Dean of Social Sciences at the University of California, Berkeley. He is co-editor (with Victoria E. Bonnell) of *Russia in the New Century: Stability or Disorder?* (Westview, 2001) and author of the forthcoming *Gorbachev and Yeltsin as Leaders* (Cambridge University Press, 2002). His earlier publications include *Khrushchev and Brezhnev as Leaders* (Allen & Unwin, 1982).

Archie Brown is Professor of Politics at the University of Oxford and Director of the Russian and East European Centre of St. Antony's College. His recent books include *The Gorbachev Factor* (Oxford University Press, 1996), *The British Study of Politics in the Twentieth Century* (co-editor with Brian Barry and Jack Hayward; Oxford University Press, 1999), and *Contemporary Russian Politics: A Reader* (editor; Oxford University Press, 2001).

Eugene Huskey is William R. Kenan, Jr. Professor of Political Science and Russian Studies at Stetson University, Florida, and the author, most recently, of *Presidential Power in Russia* (M. E. Sharpe, 1999). Among his other works on Soviet and post-Soviet politics and legal affairs are *Russian Lawyers and the Soviet State* (Princeton University Press, 1986) and *Executive Power and Soviet Politics* (editor; M. E. Sharpe, 1992).

Lilia Shevtsova is Senior Associate at the Carnegie Endowment for International Peace. Her recent publications include *Yeltsin's Russia: Myths and Reality* (Carnegie Endowment for International Peace, 1999) and (as co-author with Igor Klyamkin) *This Omnipotent and Impotent Government: The Evolution of the Political System in Post-Communist Russia* (Carnegie Moscow Center, 1999).

Carnegie Endowment for International Peace

The Carnegie Endowment is a private, nonprofit organization dedicated to advancing cooperation between nations and promoting active international engagement by the United States. Founded in 1910, its work is nonpartisan and dedicated to achieving practical results.

Through research, publishing, convening, and, on occasion, creating new institutions and international networks, Endowment associates shape fresh policy approaches. Their interests span geographic regions and the relations between governments, business, international organizations, and civil society, focusing on the economic, political, and technological forces driving global change. Through its Carnegie Moscow Center, the Endowment helps to develop a tradition of public policy analysis in the states of the former Soviet Union and to improve relations between Russia and the United States. The Endowment publishes *Foreign Policy*, one of the world's leading magazines of international politics and economics.